THE TIME-SPIRIT OF MATTHEW ARNOLD

THE TIME-SPIRIT

OF

MATTHEW ARNOLD

by

R. H. Super

Ann Arbor

The University of Michigan Press

For My Esteemed Colleagues
JOHN REVELL REINHARD
and
WARNER GRENELLE RICE

PREFACE

The lectures here published were composed at the invitation of the Harris Foundation of Northwestern University, to which (and especially to the chairman of its Lecture Committee, Professor Frederic E. Faverty) I am most grateful for the inducement to pause at the midpoint of my editorial labors upon Arnold in order to make some assessment of Arnold's achievement. It is my intention in them to show how much Arnold's work is in fact of a piece, no matter to what aspect of life he turns his attention; I hope also that I have indicated something of his relation to main currents of thought in his day and ours. Nothing is more impressive about his writing than his ability to seize upon precisely the idea or statement in the work of another writer—whether a writer he is wholeheartedly in sympathy with or one he generally disagrees with—that is most useful in formulating or expressing his views, the idea that seems most significant when regarded in the perspective of the main prospect of man's intellectual and spiritual life. (It must not be supposed, however, when I cite a passage from another writer that parallels something in Arnold, that I mean to claim that passage as his unique source; the more widely one reads, the more one discovers how widely many of these ideas—and much of this language—spread in the nineteenth century.)

This is not the book I have wanted to write about Arnold; these are not even the lectures I should have liked to give and which my kind audience was entitled to expect. They have the single advantage of being in existence, as the ideal lectures and the ideal book are not. And so with at least some sense of their shortcomings I offer them here, as I turn back to my work upon the final five volumes of Arnold's prose.

The lectures are published as they were written for delivery on April 8, 9, and 10, 1968. The tragic events of that week, however, prevented the lecture on the second of those days, and so the audience in Evanston heard on April 8 a somewhat inadequately compressed version of Lectures I and III. For thus courteously allowing their patience to be taxed, they deserve my gratitude and kindest remembrance.

The passages from the "Yale Manuscript" have been made available through the courtesy of Miss Marjorie G. Wynne, research librarian of the Beinecke Rare Book and Manuscript Library of Yale University, and are quoted by permission of the Library and of Matthew Arnold's grandson, Mr. Arnold Whitridge.

NOTE

Lectures like these depend a great deal on the scholarship
and insights of others, and it will be of service to my readers, I am confident, if I direct them to some of the best
that has been written on Arnold. For Arnold's poetry,
they will want to use the notes in Professor Kenneth Allott's edition (New York: Barnes and Noble; London:
Longmans, 1965) and *The Poetry of Matthew Arnold: A
Commentary*, by C. B. Tinker and H. F. Lowry (New
York and London: Oxford University Press, 1940). I have
alluded in my early pages to two recent books on Arnold,
G. R. Stange, *Matthew Arnold: The Poet as Humanist*
(Princeton, N.J.: Princeton University Press, 1967) and
W. A. Madden, *Matthew Arnold: A Study of the Aes-
thetic Temperament in Victorian England* (Bloomington:
Indiana University Press, 1967)—the latter unfairly, since
its value is not represented by the views I have singled out
for disagreement. The most comprehensive study of Arnold's principal poem is W. E. Houghton, "Arnold's 'Empedocles on Etna,'" *Victorian Studies* I (June, 1958),
311–36. The following studies of formative influences
upon Arnold have given me much of my material: for
Stoics and Epicureans, the chapters in Warren D. Ander-
son, *Matthew Arnold and the Classical Tradition* (Ann
Arbor: University of Michigan Press, 1965); for Emerson,

my own article, "Emerson and Arnold's Poetry," *Philological Quarterly* XXXIII (October, 1954), 396–403; for Goethe, Helen C. White's "Matthew Arnold and Goethe," *PMLA* XXXVI (September, 1921), 436–53—the first publication in a distinguished scholarly career that has recently, alas! come to an end—and J. B. Orrick, *Matthew Arnold and Goethe* (London: English Goethe Society, 1928; new series, vol. IV); for Burke, R. C. Tobias, *Matthew Arnold and Edmund Burke* (Ann Arbor, Mich.: University Microfilms, 1958); for Carlyle, Kathleen Tillotson, "Matthew Arnold and Carlyle," *Proceedings of the British Academy* XLII (1956), 133–53, and D. J. DeLaura, "Arnold and Carlyle," *PMLA* LXXIX (March, 1964), 104-29; for Mill, J. M. Robson, "Mill and Arnold: Liberty and Culture—Friends or Enemies," *Bulletin of the Canadian Humanities Association* XXXIV (Fall, 1961), 20–32, Edward Alexander, *Matthew Arnold and John Stuart Mill* (New York: Columbia University Press, 1965), and the stimulating review of that volume in the *Times Literary Supplement*, February 2, 1967, p. 90; for Dr. Arnold, E. L. Williamson, Jr., *The Liberalism of Thomas Arnold* (University, Ala.: University of Alabama Press, 1964), and for Newman, D. J. DeLaura, "Matthew Arnold and John Henry Newman: The 'Oxford Sentiment' and the Religion of the Future," *Texas Studies in Literature and Language* VI (Supplement, 1965), 571–702. There is a fine book on Arnold's religious thought, William Robbins, *The Ethical Idealism of Matthew Arnold* (Toronto: University of Toronto Press, 1959), and one forthcoming from the same publisher on the relation between Arnold's school inspecting and his social and political writings, by Fred G. Walcott. I have elsewhere publicly expressed my esteem for A. Dwight Culler's *Imaginative Reason* (New Haven: Yale University Press, 1966), though I have not drawn upon that book here. This book was already in the hands of the printer when I read Kenneth Allott's paper on "A Background for 'Empedocles on Etna,'" *Essays and*

Note

Studies XXI n.s., 80–100 (1968); the many points of correspondence between it and parts of my first lecture, even in matters of detail, are evidence of the mark Professor Allott's scholarship has long made on the modern study of Arnold. After the lectures were written, I turned again to Lionel Trilling's *Matthew Arnold* (New York: Norton, 1939) for the pleasure of rereading a truly excellent book that has not faded one jot in the three decades since its publication.

I observe that the titles of my lectures have already been used as chapter headings by my predecessors; we agree, I take it, that Arnold's own words best characterize his work.

CONTENTS

I

THE MAIN MOVEMENT OF MIND

Eighty-four years ago Matthew Arnold reached the Midwest on his lecture tour of this country, spoke twice in Chicago and once in Milwaukee. He came, unfortunately, some quarter of a century too early to benefit from the Harris Foundation, and so did not lecture in Evanston; he would have been very grateful, as I am, for its munificence. And he would have been grateful, too, for the hospitality of this university. In 1883–84 the visiting lecturer commonly depended on the hospitality of a leading spirit of the community. In Chicago, of course, this was most affluent; in the academic communities it was then not always so. Arnold himself described the president's house at Oberlin College as "the simplest and plainest living, on the whole, that [he had] seen in America,"[1] and there is still current there a story of Arnold's visit which, since I have never seen it in print, may be unfamiliar to you. Arnold was lionized at a reception, from which he prepared to retire to his room to rest and compose himself for his lecture. The president's wife asked if she could provide anything for his comfort, and he replied that he should be very glad to have some Scotch whisky. With all eyes in the room focused suddenly upon her, the president's wife collected herself and assured him that some would be forthcoming. He retired; after a considerable interval filled with activity that we can only conjecture, she knocked at his door and handed him a tray holding a bottle of Scotch—and a teaspoon.

Arnold once classified the kinds of critical judgments which might be passed upon a poet—the judgments of enthusiasm and admiration, the judgments of gratitude and sympathy, the judgment of ignorance, the judgment of incompatibility, the judgment of envy and jealousy. "Finally, there is the systematic judgment, and this judgment is the most worthless of all." For all the others may genuinely illuminate the subject. "But the systematic judgment is altogether unprofitable. Its author has not really his eye upon the professed object of his criticism at all, but upon something else which he wants to prove by means of that object."[2] Even when Arnold spoke, the worst offenders were the academics; no one in this room tonight will be in any way surprised that by now, nearly a hundred years after Arnold wrote those words, the systematizers have been hard at work on him, and that most of them bear professorial titles. Yet I should rather incline to say that the fault of most academic criticism is not systematization so much as an incurable romanticism, with its mistaken notion that poetry is self-revelation. Arnold came to poetry through the study of philosophy and the classics; art was, in his view, objective, and his poems, so far as we can surmise, began with a core of objective intellectual statement.

But a professor has been brought up from his early youth to believe that a poet is not as other men; he inhabits the unreal world of a conventional fiction, and must be discussed in terms of spiritual crises, failure of inspiration, or the like—precisely the kind of terms we should feel silly about using with respect to ourselves. And so Arnold must be viewed, in some quarters, as forever haunted by the dominating image of his great father, so that "Sohrab and Rustum" is the almost overt expression of his struggle and defeat; in other quarters as shattered by his "loss of faith"; in still others as scarred by the failure of his romance with Marguerite, the blue-eyed French girl he met on a summer holiday in Thun. And then, of course, there is the necessity of accounting for the rapid drying-up of his muse, so that after publishing two volumes of poetry in less than four years, early in 1849 and late in 1852, he with great difficulty managed to gather nine further poems for publication by the end of 1853, could add four more to his canon in the next two years, and then (except for a still-born imitation of Greek tragedy) was almost silent for over a decade. When his *New Poems* appeared in 1867, he was forty-four years old and thereafter wrote hardly a line of verse.

One can, I think, be rather cavalier with these stock conceptions, and even with the notion that the problems exist, at least in these terms. If anything seems clear about Arnold, for example, it is his pride in his father, his conviction that he is continuing in the direction his father set; and there is ample justification for his view. As for "Sohrab and Rustum," my own reading of this excellently contrived but somewhat too sentimental poem leads me to believe that, if the poem does indeed draw its emotional depth from the poet's own experience in life, it draws from his paternal pride, his wonder, his speculations about the future of his own first-born son, a one-year-old infant when he composed the poem. About Marguerite we know so little that the field for conjecture is almost unlimited; it is of course unscholarly to suggest that if there were ground for the conjectures, we might by this time have uncovered a great deal more evidence. But no one in this everyday world of ours—except a poet viewed through academic eyes—is really thought to be permanently scarred if he does not marry the first girl to whom he is attracted, and I suspect most experiences with vacation romance are best characterized in Clough's wonderfully humorous *Amours de Voyage*, written almost exactly at the same time as the "Marguerite" poems. It came as a breath of fresh air when a recent book by an academic critic treated the Marguerite poems as what they so evidently are—exercises in the craftsmanship of poetry, some of them failures, some of them brilliant successes.[3]

We might think the English teacher, brought up in the rigorous discipline of reading student papers until it seems that every spark of vital energy has been drained from him, would understand even more easily what happened to Arnold's muse. We all of us love literature, else we would not be in our profession, yet how little do we produce of creative or even critical. Surely we know from experience what Arnold meant when, late in life, he commented, "Whatever I may have once wished or intended, my life is not that of a man of letters, but of an Inspector of Schools."[4] As he looked back on his professional career, which began when he was twenty-eight years old and had published only his first volume of poetry, he remarked: "Though I am a schoolmaster's son I confess that school teaching or school inspecting is not the line of life I should naturally have chosen. I adopted it in order to marry. . . . My wife and I had a wandering life of it at first. There were but three inspectors for all England. My district went right across from Pembroke Dock to Great Yarmouth [from the westernmost tip of South Wales, that is, to the easternmost tip of East Anglia]. We had no home; one of our children was born in a lodging at Derby, with a workhouse, if I recollect right, behind and a penitentiary in front. But the irksomeness of my new duties was what I felt most, and during the first year or so this was sometimes almost insupportable."[5] So it was; a letter he wrote to his wife from an inspectoral tour begins, "I am too utterly tired out to write."[6] Other letters abundantly confirm this weariness, for the best of reasons. Yet this was the time when he was urgently looking for leisure to write "Sohrab and Rustum" and to gather a third volume of poems. Even after the traveling became less strenuous, there remained the papers to look over—spelling, arithmetic, penmanship, composition. A man can read books on the train or magazines during an afternoon break at his club, he can rise at 6:30 in the morning (while he is still young enough) to write lectures and articles, but it need strike us with no surprise that he cannot write much poetry. And when, in a brief interlude from this strenuous career, such a man can still at the age of forty-two produce a "Thyrsis," we need not, I think, talk too smugly about the drying-up of the poetic impulse.[7] The poet in Arnold, in fact, never died; passage after passage in his essays continues to show the poet's gift with language, and—an even more significant point—his whole career in poetry and prose is dominated by the kind of creative imagination that is the poet's highest virtue. His was a most remarkable perceptiveness, a fine consistency of imaginative apprehension of the world around him.

The Arnold I should like to present differs markedly, in the balance and emphasis of his traits, from the picture of him that has gradually dominated our scholarly writings—a picture that has unwittingly become a bit of a caricature. But it is less our notion of the man that I want to put in better balance than our judgment of his work, and I shall this evening deal with the man only in order to show how, in fact, his mind developed, who were his teachers, and what was his method of work as a poet. His object, almost from the start, was to grasp the spiritual essence of his age and to use his knowledge as the subject for poetry.

Much has been made of Arnold's gaiety, even frivolousness, as a schoolboy and undergraduate, and of course the love of fun remained with him throughout life, but a mere summary of his academic achievements will make clear that he was not a rebel, or at least that rebellion did not make him lose sight of the main line of academic and intellectual progress. At Rugby he won the Fifth Form Prize for Latin Verse and both the English Essay Prize and the prize for the best English poem. He ranked second of six Rugby boys who gained exhibitions at Oxford in his year, and was a scholar at Balliol College. He placed second, at Oxford, in the Hertford Latin Scholarship competition, won the Newdigate Prize for English verse, was president of the Oxford Union Society,[8] and though he took only a second class in his honors examinations in classics, won the competition for an Oriel College fellowship —in both these latter following the footsteps of his friend Clough. The atmosphere at Oxford was far more clerical than we now can easily conceive; it was a nursing ground for the clergy—two future archbishops of Canterbury were at Balliol when Arnold was there—and nearly all the permanent fellowships and a good many professorships were restricted to the clergy. We know that conversation at the scholars' table at Balliol turned often to ecclesiastical and theological matters,[9] and one of the most impressive aspects of Newman's *Apologia*, to my mind, is its remarkable account of the sort of thing that seemed important in the university about the time Arnold was there. Truly, as Arnold said, a "home of lost causes, and forsaken beliefs, and unpopular names, and impossible loyalties!"[10] Arnold's competing for the Oriel fellowship, as he did, indicates that he at least remotely entertained the notion of following an academic career that—whether at the university or in the public schools—would have involved his taking holy orders.

At the same time, of course, he was laying the ground for a career as man of letters and poet. His earliest surviving poem, written with considerable technical correctness, was composed when he was only thirteen.[11]

Again and again in his later life Arnold harks back to these Oxford days, always with warmth and affection. One of the most delightful passages in the lecture on "Emerson" which he delivered in this country in 1883–84 is his recollection of the voices in the air in those days "which haunt my memory still. Happy the man who in that susceptible season of youth hears such voices!"—the voice of Newman, still (when Arnold came to Oxford) vicar of St. Mary's; "the puissant voice of Carlyle; so sorely strained, over-used, and mis-used since, but then fresh, comparatively sound, and reaching our hearts with true, pathetic eloquence"; that "greater voice still,—the greatest voice of the century,"—who "came to us in those youthful years through Carlyle: the voice of Goethe," with its "large, liberal view of human life" and the poetry, the eloquence of *Wilhelm Meister* so perfectly caught in Carlyle's translation; and, finally, "a voice also from this side of the Atlantic,—a clear and pure voice, which for my ear, at any rate, brought a strain as new, and moving, and unforgettable, as the strain of Newman, or Carlyle, or Goethe,"—the voice of Emerson.[12] I shall say little of this last voice here. Arnold in the lecture associated Emerson with the Stoic writers he was then also reading and he described him in words almost like those he had already used for Marcus Aurelius, as "the friend and aider of those who would live in the spirit."[13] Perhaps he got from Emerson, not so much new ideas, as confirmation that he had seized rightly upon the significant current, had heeded the right ones among the multitudinous voices then in the air.

> *A voice oracular hath pealed to-day,*
> *To-day a hero's banner is unfurled,*

he wrote in an early poem, and described Emerson's message:

> *The will is free;*
> *Strong is the soul, and wise, and beautiful;*
> *The seeds of godlike power are in us still;*
> *Gods are we, bards, saints, heroes, if we will!*

When Emerson visited England in 1848, Arnold had left Oxford, but they met through Clough, and thereafter, though they seldom corresponded, Emerson and Arnold always spoke of each other in the highest terms, and Arnold's lecture on Emerson, first delivered in Boston only a year after Emerson's death, was a genuine work of piety.

Carlyle and Goethe—Goethe initially through Carlyle—saturated Arnold's mind in those days; they gave him a way of looking at the world, they gave him his notion of what was important in the world. Goethe, at least, gave him a model for his intellectual method, and Carlyle very often gave him, as we shall see, a language. The conjunction of the two sages is perhaps nowhere more clearly indicated than in one of the finest of Arnold's poems of literary criticism, the comparatively early "Memorial Verses" on the death of his father's friend Wordsworth. Using the pattern of threes that he seems so fond of in his poetry—"not this, nor this, but this"—Arnold contrasts the impact of three poets upon his own age: Byron, Goethe, and Wordsworth. Carlyle's pairing of Byron with Goethe was persistent; perhaps most memorable in *Sartor Resartus*, it occurs also in an earlier essay on Goethe, and of course it has its origin in Goethe's own great interest in Byron and Byronism. "Byron's life-weariness, his moody melancholy, and mad stormful indignation, borne on the tones of a wild and quite artless melody, [pierced] deep into many a British heart," wrote Carlyle. "Byron was our English Sentimentalist and Power-man; the strongest of his kind in Europe; the wildest, the gloomiest, and it may be hoped the last." "Among our own poets, Byron was almost the only man we saw faithfully and manfully struggling to the end, in [the] cause [of the moral and spiritual freedom of mankind]; and he died while the victory was still doubtful, or at best, only beginning to be gained. . . . Goethe's success in this matter has been more complete than that of any other man in his age."[14] Arnold wrote of Byron:

> *He taught us little; but our soul*
> *Had felt him like the thunder's roll.*

> *With shivering heart the strife we saw*
> *Of passion with eternal law;*
> *And yet with reverential awe*
> *We watched the fount of fiery life*
> *Which served for that Titanic strife.*

But the link between Wordsworth and Goethe is also in Carlyle's essay: "Goethe . . . appears to us as a person of that deep endowment, and gifted vision, of that experience also and sympathy in the ways of all men, which qualify him to stand forth, not only as the literary ornament, but in many respects too as the Teacher and exemplar of his age. For, to say nothing of his natural gifts, he has cultivated himself and his art, he has studied how to live and to write, with a fidelity, an unwearied earnestness, of which there is no other living instance; of which, among British poets especially, Wordsworth alone offers any resemblance." Carlyle speaks of "the spirit in which [Goethe] cultivates his Art; the noble, disinterested, almost religious love with which he looks on Art in general, and strives towards it as towards the sure, highest, nay, only good." "His peace is not from blindness, but from clear vision; . . . he has inquired fearlessly, and fearlessly searched out and denied the False; but he has not forgotten, what is equally essential and infinitely harder, to search out and admit the True."[15]

> *Physician of the iron age,*
> *Goethe has done his pilgrimage.*
> *He took the suffering human race,*
> *He read each wound, each weakness clear;*
> *And struck his finger on the place,*
> *And said:* Thou ailest here, and here!
> *He looked on Europe's dying hour*
> *Of fitful dream and feverish power;*
> *His eye plunged down the weltering strife,*
> *The turmoil of expiring life—*

He said: The end is everywhere,
Art still has truth, take refuge there! [16]*

In 1847 or early 1848 Arnold bought himself, for £8
10s, the 55-volume set of Goethe's works published at
Stuttgart under the author's direction, and immediately
plunged into the *Autobiography*, from which he translated copiously into a notebook he was keeping.[17] It could
hardly be asserted that he governed his own judgment of
books by Goethe's, but Goethe certainly confirmed his
sense of the importance of the Stoics, of Lessing's *Laoc-
oon*, and of Spinoza, and may, indeed, have introduced
him to the two last. "The two things which are most remarkable about [Spinoza], and by which, as I think, he
chiefly impressed Goethe," Arnold later wrote, are "his
denial of final causes, and his stoicism, a stoicism not pas-
sive, but active. For a mind like Goethe's,—a mind profoundly impartial and passionately aspiring after the
science, not of men only, but of universal nature,—the
popular philosophy which explains all things by reference
to man, and regards universal nature as existing for the sake
of man, and even of certain classes of men, was utterly re-
pulsive. . . . Creation, he thought, should be made of
sterner stuff. . . . More than any philosopher who has ever
lived, Spinoza satisfied [Goethe] here." And Arnold
quotes from Spinoza's *Tractatus Theologico-Politicus:*
"God directs nature, according as the universal laws of
nature, but not according as the particular laws of human
nature require; and so God has regard, not of the human
race only, but of entire nature." Then Arnold summarizes
Spinoza's stoicism: "Our desire is not that nature may
obey us, but, on the contrary, that we may obey nature."
"Here is the second source of his attractiveness for
Goethe; and Goethe is but the eminent representative of a

*When the superscript number is printed in italics, as here,
the note to which it refers contains something beyond the mere
indication of the source of a statement or quotation.

whole order of minds whose admiration has made Spinoza's fame. Spinoza first impresses Goethe and any man like Goethe, and then he composes him; first he fills and satisfies his imagination by the width and grandeur of his view of nature, and then he fortifies and stills his mobile, straining, passionate, poetic temperament by the moral lesson he draws from his view of nature. And a moral lesson not of mere resigned acquiescence, not of melancholy quietism, but of joyful activity within the limits of man's true sphere." [18] In Carlyle's view, the main significance of Goethe for the modern world was religious—"the beautiful, the religious Wisdom, which may still, with something of its old impressiveness, speak to the whole soul; still, in these hard, unbelieving utilitarian days, reveal to us glimpses of the Unseen but not unreal World, that so the Actual and the Ideal may again meet together, and clear Knowledge be again wedded to Religion, in the life and business of man." [19]

Two years after his election to the Oriel fellowship, Arnold took a position as private secretary to one of the senior Whig statesmen, Lord Lansdowne, then Lord President of the Privy Council, and he moved to London. Whether this was meant to be the first step in a career in politics or the civil service is not certain; it was certainly a firm step away from an academic career, though he retained his Oriel fellowship for another four years. But although the new post gave Arnold an intimate view of the operations of the government, and although he was very much stirred by the revolution of 1848—which Clough witnessed at first hand in Paris—his most passionate concern was poetry. The correspondence with Clough especially set him to reflecting on the nature and function of poetry in these "damned times"—for Clough sent poem after poem for Arnold's criticism and published two volumes in three months, November, 1848, and January, 1849. [20] Arnold seems to have been less eager to invite Clough's criticism, for though by the latter date his own first book was only a month away, there had been little evidence of his creative activity in the Clough correspondence.

The critical doctrines his letters enunciate are somewhat groping and confused; they are undeveloped and incomplete, as one might expect in short and informal letters, and in some instances they are couched in language meant to be helpful and inoffensive to Clough, rather than absolute pronouncements. In any case, we see an inclination to praise a natural rather than an ornate style, a concern for "naturalness—i.e., an absolute propriety—of form, as the sole *necessary* of Poetry as such," and a sense of the need for taking a central intellectual position within one's age: poets "must begin with an Idea of the world in order not to be prevailed over by the world's multitudinousness: or if they cannot get that, at least with isolated ideas: and all other things shall (perhaps) be added unto them." But the poet's primary business is *pleasure;* it is as fatal for him to try to "*solve* the Universe" as to "dawdle with its painted shell." "In a *man* style is the saying in the best way *what you have to say.* The *what you have to say* depends on your age. . . . The poet's matter being *the hitherto experience of the world, and his own,* increases with every century. . . . For me, you may often hear my sinews cracking under the effort to unite matter. . . ."[21]

Arnold's first volume, *The Strayed Reveller and Other Poems*, published on February 26, 1849, reflects in some measure the discussion in the letters. We have little evidence about the writing of the poems. The sonnet on Shakespeare survives in a manuscript dated "1 Aug. 1844," "Stagirius" in one dated simply "1844," and Arnold's younger brother Thomas believed that the others were written over a considerable span of years.[22] There is real danger, however, in dating a poem, as he does, from the date of the biographical event it celebrates: "Resignation," for example, uses as its setting a walk through the Lake District that took place in July, 1843, when Arnold was twenty,[23] yet that is surely—if one may judge by the maturity of thought and grasp of style and form—far too early a date; the intellectual problem of the poem is not that of a twenty-year-old. I incline to think that most of the volume's eleven sonnets and sixteen other poems were composed not long before publication—in 1848, probably. They were the work of a young poet learning his craft. He tried fifteen quite different verse-forms in the sixteen poems that were not sonnets; only "The Hayswater Boat" and "A Memory Picture" use somewhat similar stanzas. The sonnets, too, are clearly practice pieces; he scarcely used the form again until his last collection in 1867. The poem "Resignation," in particular, shows the mastery of structure that Arnold learned from the "conversation poems" of Wordsworth and Coleridge, a structure he used again in some of the best poems of his maturity. "The Strayed Reveller" and "The New Sirens" deal directly with poetic theory, and their titles, like that of "Mycerinus," show an early inclination (for which he was much criticized) to use classical story as a vehicle for modern thought. Many of the poems are not doctrinal, but to the extent that any doctrine pervades the book, it is stoicism, directly praised in the sonnet "To a Friend" and reflected in such poems as the Emersonian "Quiet Work," the sonnet on Shakespeare, "Mycerinus,"[24] "The Sick King in Bokhara," "The World and the Quietist," and, most important, in "Resignation." The favorite of Arnold's readers then, as perhaps now, was "The Forsaken Merman"; the poem in which he himself seems to have been most interested, and the one that looked most clearly in the direction he was to follow in his next volume, was "Resignation," with which the book ends. It has always struck me as noteworthy that Arnold placed this and his next volume in the hands of his father's publisher—not a publisher of poetry, that is, but a publisher of sermons.[25]

His poetic impulse was if anything spurred to greater intensity by the success of getting a volume published;

within a few months Arnold was hard at work on "Empedocles on Etna," a poem which in his own view was merely a sort of preliminary study to the *chef d'oeuvre* he never actually got round to writing, the tragedy of "Lucretius." In April, 1851, he accepted from Lord Lansdowne the appointment as inspector of schools, married in June, now at last resigned his Oriel fellowship, and in November, 1853, proceeded to the degree of M.A. he had so long neglected to take; presumably it was needed to lend dignity to his inspectorship.

There exists a sheaf of papers of various sizes and shapes, for the most part sheets of letter paper, that some modern collector has mounted in an elegant morocco scrapbook and that is now somewhat misleadingly known as the "Yale Manuscript"—misleadingly, because, as I have said, the papers were merely accumulated refuse from Arnold's writing desk, neither a notebook nor, in any sense of unity, a manuscript.[26] One leaf bears the holograph inscription "M. Arnold Ball: Coll: 1843," though there is perhaps no connection between that inscription and the rest of the contents of the sheet; another leaf preserves a brief memorandum written while Arnold was Lord Lansdowne's secretary, and therefore cannot be earlier than 1847. A number of leaves contain stanzas of Empedocles' philosophical song in Arnold's drama, and there are some verses of "Tristram and Iseult," both poems published in 1852. It is probably not amiss to guess that many of these leaves were written about 1849 and that they represent, in fact, something of Arnold's attempt to reach the sort of "Idea of the World" he conceived essential for the poet.[27]

What are some of these jottings?

A man may fall into spiritual distress at 2 periods of the world. Either at a period when the belief in a God is (generally) universal—

or

when, tho: prevalent among the vulgar, this belief is amongst thinkers losing ground.———

at the first period the issue from spiritual distress will be probably to fervent religion:

——at the second to a mastery over oneself & the world.

Confusion arises from taking the step out of harmony with the period.

Bruno—Maurice

in England where the movement of the world is not known or observed the wrong step may be repeatedly taken.[28]

a God identical with the world and with the sum of being & force therein contained: not exterior to it, possessing being & force exterior to it, and determining it *à son gré.*[29]

We learn not to *abuse* or *storm at* the Gods or Fate: knowing this mere madness: as there is nothing wilfully operating against us—the only object of anger: and the power we would curse is the same with ourselves: the same with the tongue employed to articulate the curse. God patiently lends himself to curse himself.[30]

what a thing it is to have a reason in oneself for doing or not doing a thing and how few have experienced it.

——every time we approach philosophy we test it by our hitherto acquired experience. It is better therefore to approach it late.[31]

We have been on a thousand lines & on each have shown spirit, talent, even geniality but hardly for an hour between birth & death have we been on our own, one natural line, have we been ourselves, have we breathed freely.

only that which recalls a whole can refresh him who looks upon a whole. Tennyson has the naïveté of language & image—but not the large plain manner of thinking & feeling that is in nature—the Greek philosophers (Epicurus Empedocles &c) have the great way of thinking coextensive with nature, & not fantastically individual, but not the relief of the naïveté of Nature—with its landscapes & affections. Homer & the Old Testament & on the whole Shakspeare unite both.

——Epicureanism is Stoical, & there is no theory of life but is[32]

The Roman World perished for having disobeyed reason and nature.

The infancy of the world was renewed with all its sweet illusions

but infancy and its illusions must for ever be transitory, and we are again in the place of the Roman world, our illusions past, debtors to the service of reason & nature.

O let us beware how we again are false to them: we shall perish, and the world will be renewed: but we shall leave the same question to be solved by a future age.

——I cannot conceal from myself the objection which really wounds & perplexes me from the religious side is that the service of reason is freezing to feeling, chilling to the religious mood. & feeling & the religious mood are eternally the deepest being of man, the ground of all joy & greatness for him.

The misery of the present age is not in the intensity of men's suffering—but in their incapacity to suffer, enjoy, feel at all, wholly & profoundly—in their having their susceptibility eternally agacée by a continual dance of ever-changing objects, and not having the power to attach it upon one, to expend it on that one, to absorb it in that one: in their being ever learning & never coming to the knowledge of the truth: in their having a presentiment of all things, a possession of none: in their having one moment the commencement of a feeling, at the next moment the commencement of an imagination, at the next the commencement of a thought & the eternal tumult of the world mingling, breaking in upon, hurrying away all. Deep suffering is the consciousness of oneself—no less than deep enjoyment. The dream of the present age is Divorce from oneself.

If every one would mend one[33]

—Well they cry we have mended one: and we must now cry aloud, till we mend you & the world.

—I will not ask, are you sure you are mended in this or that particular? but I will ask, are you sufficient for that new, that self-contained, abundant life, which we should be mended into. This crusade, this attacking state, is abnormal temporary: it occupies Existence with the same stimulus of noise & outward action, the cowardly self-betaking whereto has been the source of the meanness & blindness of all those you would mend: are you sure that, with you, beneath the hot outside, reposes a capacity of substantial life?

Fragments though these are, jottings on scraps of paper, they all tend in much the same direction and they are recognizably the foundation of some of Arnold's most important poems. Moreover, though these jottings (as I have said) seem to have been made in the late 1840's or very early 1850's, one of them is almost a summary of "Obermann Once More," a poem that cannot have been begun earlier than 1865. From the time Arnold actually took his intellectual position, his view of the world remained remarkably consistent.

The pivotal poem in Arnold's career is of course "Empedocles on Etna"; now uniformly regarded as his most important work, and regarded at least in some quarters as the most important longer poem of the Victorian period, it was discarded by the author himself after its first publication and only made its reappearance some fifteen years later. Not only did he discard it, he wrote a Preface of some length to explain why he discarded it. Here the modern critics have been in their element. Arnold, they say, revealed too much of himself in "Empedocles"; having actually produced "an allegory of the state of his own mind" (to use his own phrase), he stepped back and repudiated what he had done, even denied somewhat hotly that he had done it, and took refuge in the cold objectivity of a pair of factitious pseudo-epics from Persian and from Norse legend. Arnold's phrase "the dialogue of the mind with itself" becomes, for such critics, the poet's private, divided mind. "As a projection of his own central experience, 'Empedocles on Etna' is Arnold's greatest achievement," says one of the best of the modern academics,[34] and lest we should doubt what he means by Arnold's "own central experience," he tells us further: "Forced to choose between a stoic life of resignation and suicide, Arnold in real life chose resignation; Empedocles' suicide, as he later remarked, was not a course of action literally recommended in the poem."[35] I wish I were sure that the author of that statement, whom I know and admire, intended it to be humorous. For it is, in fact, representative of a point of view that entirely misjudges both what Arnold intended and what he achieved. The critic has listened too willingly to the song of the New Sirens and has equated "knowledge" with "feeling."

First a word about the Preface to *Poems* (1853) in which Arnold explains why he has discarded "Empedocles." He insists at the outset that the subject of the poem was entirely appropriate and that he did not, in his own judgment, fail in the delineation which he intended to effect. The age of Empedocles was very much like the modern era; it was an age when the old religious vision was fading, the influence of the Sophists was sowing the seed of doubt without providing the wholeness of consolation. "The calm, the cheerfulness, the disinterested objectivity [of the older Greek literature] have disappeared; the dialogue of the mind with itself has commenced; modern problems have presented themselves; we hear already the doubts, we witness the discouragement, of Hamlet and of Faust." This statement, be it noted, is presented as an objective diagnosis of the central intellectual characteristic of the modern era, not as a purely private, essentially emotional approach to life. The play adds, he asserts, "to our knowledge." Such an objective diagnosis of its ills, however, the modern age seems not to want, Arnold continues. It wants one of two things: it wants introspection, "a true allegory of the state of one's own mind," or it wants glorification of its own achievements—it wants its poets to "inflate themselves with a belief in the pre-eminent importance and greatness of their own times," and to this latter function it gives the modest name of "interpreting their age": in the context it is perfectly clear that "interpreting" means "praising" and nothing else.[36] By implication, Arnold denies that "Empedocles on Etna" followed either of these false lights, and I venture to suggest that in this respect he knew better than his modern critics.

Our principal source of information about the historical Empedocles is Diogenes Laertius, and a glance at his account may give some clue to Arnold's reason for seeing in Empedocles the type-figure of the modern dilemma. Once Arnold made his choice, it must be remembered, some parts of the story were beyond his control: he could provide motives for the suicide and analyze the frame of mind that led to it, but he could not evade the suicide; the suicide, that is to say, is particular to the donnée, not an alternative advanced by Arnold in his analysis of himself or his age. The story as Diogenes Laertius gives it, is this:

Empedocles was a native of Agrigentum, in Sicily, an admirer and perhaps pupil of Parmenides. Aristotle later described him as the inventor of rhetoric and as a poet of Homer's school, powerful in diction, great in metaphors and in the use of all other poetical devices. He was an excellent orator, with great political power in his native city as champion of the people against the tyrants. Exiled on political grounds, he was soon much regretted by his fellow citizens, though his return continued to be opposed by his personal enemies. His skill as a physician led some of his disciples to attribute to him feats of magic, such as raising the woman Pantheia from the dead (although other accounts said he cured her from a trance after she was given up by the doctors). He is said to have disclosed the secret of this cure to his friend the physician Pausanias, son of Anchitus. On one occasion, after a feast at the home of Peisianax, the company retired to rest, some under the trees, others wherever they chose, leaving Empedocles on his couch at table. At daybreak he was missing. One of the company reported that in the middle of the night he had heard an exceedingly loud voice calling Empedocles, and that he then beheld a light in the heavens and the glitter of lamps. Pausanias at first sent people to search for him, but later bade them take no further trouble, for things beyond expectation had happened: Empedocles was now a god and it was their duty to sacrifice to him. In more sober fact, when Empedocles got up from his couch, he set out for Etna, plunged into the fiery crater and disappeared—presumably, by leaving no traces of his body, to give ground for the report that he had been deified. One of his poems makes this claim:

> I walk among you, no longer a mortal, but an immortal god, reverenced by all, as is meet, crowned with fillets and flowery garlands. Straightway I enter into flourishing towns, I am reverenced by men and women, and myriads follow me, eager to learn where is the path which leads to salvation, some desirous of oracles, others, long tortured by all kinds of diseases, longing to hear the sweet sounding word of healing.[37]

This, then, is the story Arnold uses. Empedocles' motive for the leap, of course, must be changed, since it is ridiculous, not tragic, and in one of the leaves of the so-called Yale Manuscript Arnold devotes a good deal of space to an analysis of the motive—a document that can hardly, one would think, be understood as self-analysis on Arnold's part. Ultimately, Arnold writes there, in the conflict between the severity and stern simplicity of Empedocles' intellect and the sense of defeat and isolation in his life, "his spring and elasticity of mind are gone: he is clouded, oppressed, dispirited, without hope & energy. Before he becomes the victim of depression & overtension of mind, to the utter deadness to joy, grandeur, spirit, and animated life, he desires to die; to be reunited with the universe, before by exaggerating his human side he has become utterly estranged from it."[38] For this line of reasoning, classical stoicism gives its justification: death is the common human condition, which no man can avoid; if then the external forces of the world are so great that one can live only by sacrificing one's integrity of spirit, it is better to choose death while one preserves his integrity than to meet that inevitable death after one has surrendered. Even Socrates, who spoke vigorously against suicide, appeared to Epictetus to have chosen death when he remained in Athens and refused to make the moral compromises his persecutors demanded of him. A letter Arnold wrote in 1867 has often been quoted as an authoritative confutation of the view that the doctrine of the poem is fundamentally stoic: "No critic appears to remark that if Empedocles throws himself into Etna his creed can hardly be meant to be one to live by. If the creed of Empedocles were, as exhibited in my poem, a satisfying one, he ought to have lived after delivering himself of it, not died."[39] But scholars have paid too little attention to the identity of Arnold's correspondent—a rather humorless man who a few years later pamphleteered against *Literature and Dogma*. It looks to me as though the letter was merely courteously fobbing off a somewhat impertinent questioner who was hardly worth a detailed argument he could not understand. Poets are seldom fond of explaining in prose what their poems "mean." In fact, the inability of Empedocles, under the particular conditions of his life, to live up to his creed is no more a condemnation of the creed than is the inability of Christians to live up to theirs: the creed remains an ideal which it is better the world should have, should strive to live by. The founder of Christianity, like Socrates, died rather than repudiate his creed.[40]

Much has been written, and excellently written, about the intellectual content of "Empedocles on Etna"— its remarkable combination of Stoic ethics and Epicurean or Lucretian theology; much too has been well said about the poem as an analysis of the spiritual condition of Victorian England, in which "littleness united Is become invincible." One aspect of the poem has not caught the eye as it should have, however, and that is its relation to the popular Christianity of the nineteenth century. When Empedocles says, "Be neither saint nor sophist led, but be a man!" (I, ii, 136), the saints parallel the Evangelicals and Protestant Dissenters, the sophists parallel the eudaemonist rationalists, the Utilitarians. And the man who is believed to have raised another from the dead and who scorns to deny it, the man who, when he is about to die, tells his disciple,

> Either to-morrow or some other day,
> In the sure revolutions of the world,
> Good friend, I shall revisit Catana

—this man has invited, perhaps unwittingly, the very kind of superstitious regard for himself with which in Arnold's view Christian dogma had surrounded Jesus, for here are the seeds of miracles like the raising of Lazarus and the resurrection of Jesus himself.[41]

> Ask not what days and nights
> In trance Pantheia lay,
> But ask how thou such sights
> May'st see without dismay;
> Ask what most helps when known, thou son of Anchitus!

says Empedocles. One witty critic has remarked that Pausanias, as a physician, had a professional interest in learning the secret of raising Pantheia from the dead;[42]

Empedocles, however, puts his finger on the essential matter of any such story—even the resurrected Lazarus died
sometime, and man's problem is not how to postpone
death, but how to accommodate his mind to the sure
knowledge that it will come, for himself, for his friends,
for all mankind. Among the theologies Arnold's Empedocles ridicules is the popular Christian notion of a personal
god and a life in heaven that fulfills those lacks we have
felt in this life.[43]

Arnold's principal addition to the Empedocles story
was the youth Callicles, the lad who sees still all the natural magic of nature, whose intuition leads him to insights
as true as and far fresher than those achieved by Empedocles' powerful mind. We today are likely to associate
Callicles with the Wordsworth of Arnold's "Memorial
Verses"; one of Arnold's memoranda from the Yale Manuscript makes another association—the memorandum that
contrasts Tennyson's naïveté of language and image with
the stern intellectual grandeur of Epicurus and Empedocles, and opposes both partial views to writers like Homer
who unite the two. "Only that which recalls a whole can
refresh him who looks upon a whole," that memorandum
began, and it reminds us of Arnold's comment upon Sophocles, that "He saw life steadily and saw it whole." The
allusion of the memorandum is, I take it, to the early Tennyson, who "dawdled with the painted shell of the Universe," yet in whose school Arnold's generation had inevitably been brought up,[44] who like Callicles felt the
vitality not only of external nature but of antique myth.[45]

Wholeness, then, Arnold hoped to achieve by the balance of Callicles and Empedocles. The artist in him perceived also the need for some elevation at the end, to re-
deem the gloom of the hero, and so Empedocles dies in a
moment of ecstasy, seeing that death at this moment will
be the salvation of a soul that might otherwise be lost forever. (The historic Empedocles believed in the transmi-
gration of souls.) But neither artistic device satisfied Ar-

nold's critical sense. Nor could he take much satisfaction in his contemporaries' understanding what the poem was about—when a reviewer found in it a concoction of Carlyle, Comte, and Sainte-Beuve;[46] the analysis of his age was too obscure for the age to recognize itself. And so, on grounds that were entirely warranted by the poem's reception, Arnold set aside the work, as one that lacked plot, that depended on a situation "in which a continuous state of mental distress is prolonged, unrelieved by incident, hope, or resistance; in which there is everything to be endured, nothing to be done."[47] The decision was a rigorous one, and I will not say it was not perverse; it does seem to me to have been completely honest.

"Empedocles on Etna" is an analysis of the spiritual state, the religious state, of the mid-nineteenth century. So too were some other of Arnold's most characteristic poems; indeed, the analysis became more overt as he moved from "Empedocles" to "The Scholar-Gipsy" in 1853, "Stanzas from the Grande Chartreuse" in 1855, "Dover Beach" (as I should incline to think) also about 1855, and finally "Obermann Once More" in 1865–67. The most complex is the "Grande Chartreuse": here the old faith interacts with the rationalism that aspired to the "high white star of Truth," and the modern technological materialists—those who "give the universe their law," who "triumph over time and space" through (one may suppose) such gadgets as the steam locomotive and the electric telegraph—interact with those who long for spiritual qualities the age cannot give, and the complexity becomes almost more than we can sort out.[48] Once again scraps from the Yale Manuscript contain the seeds of the poem. The note, "The misery of the present age is not in the intensity of men's suffering—but in their incapacity to suffer, enjoy, feel at all, wholly & profoundly," becomes the magnificent line,

The nobleness of grief is gone.

And the continuation of this memorandum, with its picture of men moving from the commencement of a feeling to the commencement of an imagination to the commencement of a thought, links this passage of the "Grande Chartreuse" to "The Scholar-Gipsy," in which the ills of the age are summed up in the line,

> *From change to change their being rolls.*

The memorandum on the reformers—those who, thinking they have mended themselves, now must cry aloud till they mend us and the world—leads to the stanza on the "sciolists":

> *For the world cries your faith is now*
> *But a dead time's exploded dream;*
> *My melancholy, sciolists say,*
> *Is a past mode, an outworn theme—*
> *As if the world had ever had*
> *A faith, or sciolists been sad!*

Carlyle used the word "sciolists" in much the same context in *Sartor Resartus*.[49] Indeed, his analysis of the age in the essay "Characteristics" (1831) is behind a good deal of this poem: "Hard, for the most part, is the fate of such men; the harder the nobler they are. In dim forecastings, wrestles within them the 'Divine Idea of the World,' yet will nowhere visibly reveal itself. They have to realise a Worship for themselves, or live unworshipping. The Godlike has vanished from the world; and they, by the strong cry of their soul's agony, like true wonder-workers, must again evoke its presence. This miracle is their appointed task; which they must accomplish, or die wretchedly: this miracle has been accomplished by such; but not in our land; our land yet knows not of it. Behold a Byron, in melodious tones, 'cursing his day': he mistakes earth-born passionate Desire for heaven-inspired Freewill; without heavenly loadstar, rushes madly into the dance of me-

teoric lights that hover on the mad Mahlstrom; and goes
down among its eddies. Hear a Shelley filling the earth
with inarticulate wail; like the infinite, inarticulate grief
and weeping of forsaken infants."[50]

> *What helps it now, that Byron bore,*
> *With haughty scorn which mocked the smart,*
> *Through Europe to the Aetolian shore*
> *The pageant of his bleeding heart?*
> *That thousands counted every groan,*
> *And Europe made his woe her own?*
>
> *What boots it, Shelley! that the breeze*
> *Carried thy lovely wail away,*
> *Musical through Italian trees*
> *Which fringe thy soft blue Spezzian bay?*
> *Inheritors of thy distress*
> *Have restless hearts one throb the less?*

Again from Carlyle's "Characteristics": "To the better order of such minds any mad joy of Denial has long
since ceased: the problem is not now to deny, but to ascer-
tain and perform. Once in destroying the False, there was
a certain inspiration; but now the genius of Destruction
has done its work, there is now nothing more to destroy.
The doom of the Old has long been pronounced, and ir-
revocable; the Old has passed away: but, alas, the New appears not in its stead; the Time is still in pangs of travail
with the New. Man has walked by the light of conflagra-
tions, and amid the sound of falling cities; and now there
is darkness, and long watching till it be morning. The
voice even of the faithful can but exclaim: 'As yet strug-
gles the twelfth hour of the Night: birds of darkness are
on the wing, spectres uproar, the dead walk, the living
dream.—Thou, Eternal Providence, wilt cause the day to
dawn!' "[51]

> *Wandering between two worlds, one dead,*
> *The other powerless to be born,*

is the way Arnold describes the spiritual condition of his day in "Grande Chartreuse";

> *We are here as on a darkling plain*
> *Swept with confused alarms of struggle and flight,*
> *Where ignorant armies clash by night,*

in "Dover Beach."

"A man may fall into spiritual distress," you will remember from the Yale Manuscript, "when the belief in a God, though prevalent among the vulgar, is amongst thinkers losing ground." Under such circumstances, a proper apprehension of the condition will lead "to a mastery over oneself and the world." But an improper apprehension will lead to such flounderings (Arnold cites his example) as those of Frederick Denison Maurice, "that pure and devout spirit," as Arnold called him in *Literature and Dogma*, "of whom, however, the truth must at last be told, that in theology he passed his life beating the bush with deep emotion and never starting the hare."[52] "In England," the Yale Memorandum continues, "where the movement of the world is not known or observed the wrong step may be repeatedly taken."

For the solitary, sensitive man the spiritual state of England is indeed distressing. But it is not one for despair. The central metaphor to describe the state of England in "Grande Chartreuse" is that of a wanderer between two worlds, one dead, the other powerless to be born; the central metaphor for it in "Dover Beach" is of the "Sea of Faith," of which now one only hears

> *Its melancholy, long, withdrawing roar,*
> *Retreating, to the breath*
> *Of the night-wind, down the vast edges drear*
> *And naked shingles of the world.*

I am not sure how far a poet may be held to the implications of his metaphors, but both of these might be taken in fact to imply that the remedy lies with time. No foetus ever has power to be born of its own will, but when the fullness of time comes it is born; the tide which once brightly engulfed and embraced the shore and reflected the moonlight will once again, inevitably, be back, "various, beautiful, new, with joy, with love, with light, with certitude, with peace, with help for pain." And it is precisely the tidal image that Arnold uses to convey the notion of a new, a vital religious impulse, in "Obermann Once More." That era of splendid material accomplishment, the last days of the Roman republic and the first days of the empire, that era of spiritual desiccation so devastatingly represented by Lucretius, was, Arnold tells us in this poem (as he had already told his Oxford audience in 1857), very like Victorian England; upon this world Christianity was born, and the world heeded its message—"Seek in thy soul for the satisfaction of thy longings." For centuries Christ was kept alive in the hearts of men; wherever men believed, he was present. Now he is dead:

> *that tide of common thought,*
> *Which bathed our life, retired;*
> *Slow, slow the old world wore to nought,*
> *And pulse by pulse expired.*

In Obermann's hour, that of the French Revolution, "the old was out of date, The new was not yet born." But now, as Arnold writes, "The world's great order dawns in sheen"—and the poet, now past the middle of his life, is admonished:

> *What still of strength is left, employ*
> *That end to help attain:*
> One common wave of thought and joy
> Lifting mankind again!

The poems I have been talking about this evening are complex intellectually, complex in the interplay of mind and emotion. To take them as self-expression, as personal, is, I think, to mis-take them; they are representative, not individual, in the emotion they express. Only by understanding them thus can we understand what Arnold himself was getting at when he wrote of his complete body of poetry, "My poems represent, on the whole, the main movement of mind of the last quarter of a century, and thus they will probably have their day as people become conscious to themselves of what that movement of mind is, and interested in the literary productions which reflect it. It might be fairly urged that I have less poetical sentiment than Tennyson, and less intellectual vigour and abundance than Browning; yet, because I have perhaps more of a fusion of the two than either of them, and have more regularly applied that fusion to the main line of modern development, I am likely enough to have my turn, as they have had theirs."[53] The main movement of mind—to simplify a great deal too much—was a combination of Carlyle's analysis of the state of England, Goethe's catholicity and disinterestedness, and Spinoza's firm grasp of the true relation between man and the universe, of the true essence of the Old and the New Testaments.

II

THE LIBERAL OF THE FUTURE

Newman's *Apologia* is the record of a war against Liberalism, and Newman's list of eighteen typical propositions of Liberalism—propositions which, praise God! he had not held—is entertaining and illuminating reading. For example:

> 2. No one can believe what he does not understand. Therefore, e.g., there are no mysteries in true religion.
> 3. No theological doctrine is any thing more than an opinion which happens to be held by bodies of men. Therefore, e.g., no creed, as such, is necessary for salvation.
> 17. The people are the legitimate source of power. Therefore, e.g., Universal Suffrage is among the natural rights of man.
> 18. Virtue is the child of knowledge, and vice of ignorance. Therefore, e.g., education, periodical literature, railroad travelling, ventilation, drainage, and the arts of life, when fully carried out, serve to make a population moral and happy.[1]

It would seem that no matter by which road one approached Liberalism, one got to the same place. And though not every nineteenth-century Liberal held all liberal doctrines in all fields equally, there can be no doubt that a good many of the doctrines did meet in Arnold's father, and that Matthew Arnold himself was brought up in an atmosphere that combined free inquiry into religious matters with allegiance to the political party that nominated Dr. Arnold to the Professorship of Modern History at Oxford, the political party that later took Matthew Arnold from the theologically liberal atmosphere of Oriel College to become private secretary to one of its most influential leaders and finally to a post as Inspector of Schools.

Arnold's first nineteen years in London were the hey-day of Liberal prosperity, challenged only by two very short Tory administrations under the Earl of Derby —the one lasting only ten months in 1852, the other sixteen months in 1858–59; unfortunately, they were not years in which the greatest talents of the country seemed to be at the helm. The letters Arnold wrote to Clough from Lansdowne House showed a resolute attempt to avoid political involvement, but whenever his interest in political matters became overpowering, his letters showed also a strong sense of the inadequacy of the Whig leaders.

But if he struggled with himself to keep from reading the newspapers, he came out of the decade of the forties with a number of convictions about the function of government and the course of the political history of England and Europe that were much at odds with the run-of-the-mill political liberalism of his day. The same notebook into which he transcribed long extracts from Goethe's *Autobiography* contains nearly as many pages taken from Burke's correspondence.[2] Burke in political matters became for Arnold almost what Newman became in religious affairs—a man of extraordinary intellectual talent in his field, a man who, "almost alone in England, . . . brings thought to bear upon politics," whose writings, "for those who can make the needful corrections," are distinguished by "their profound, permanent, fruitful, philosophical truth."[3] The needful corrections must be made, however, as with Newman, because of the vast alteration in the entire climate of opinion that had taken place since Burke and Newman formed their views. The most fruitful conception Arnold seems to have drawn from Burke—though the words apparently are not Burke's—is that of the modern State as the people "themselves in their collective and corporate character," "their collective best selves," as Arnold frequently puts it.[4] And Burke's most memorable remark, to Arnold's mind, is that which he held up as the model of intelligence and disinterestedness—a passage from *Thoughts on French Affairs* in December, 1791, in which, after reaffirming with full vigor his conviction that the revolution was fraught with evil, Burke could nevertheless conclude: "If a great change is to be made in human affairs, the minds of men will be fitted to it; the general opinions and feelings will draw that way. Every fear, every hope will forward it; and then they who persist in opposing this mighty current in human affairs, will appear rather to resist the decrees of Providence itself, than the mere designs of men. They will not be resolute and firm, but perverse and obstinate." "That return of Burke upon himself," commented Arnold, "has always seemed to me one of the finest things in English literature, or indeed in any literature. That is what I call living by ideas: when one side of a question has long had your earnest support, when all your feelings are engaged, when you hear all round you no language but one, when your party talks this language like a steam-engine and can imagine no other,—still to be able to think, still to be irresistibly carried, if it so be, by the current of thought to the opposite side of the question, and, like Balaam, to be unable to speak anything *but what the Lord has put in your mouth*. I know nothing more striking, and I must add that I know nothing more un-English."[5]

We have seen that at the beginning of his inspectoral career, when his primary longing was still to be a poet,

Arnold found the drudgery of his new duties almost intolerable. It became tolerable as he came round to the view that the cause of public education was one important area in which English political and social life might be made effectively to harmonize with the main current of the "modern spirit," with (as he came to call it) the *Zeitgeist*. That spirit, as Arnold saw it, was epitomized by the French Revolution, itself the culmination of forces long at work in Europe; destructive of the old creeds and the old social order, which collapsed before its force, the Revolution and its ideas were preserved on the Continent by the administrative genius of the Napoleonic government. In England the old order survived a little longer—long enough to win the victory of Waterloo. "But with the victory of Waterloo the period for endurance and resistance, for the great qualities of an aristocracy, ended: the period for intelligent reconstruction, for the application of ideas, for the exercise of faculties in which an aristocracy is weak, arrived,"[6] Arnold remarked in his first political pamphlet, almost his first published prose. The great victor of Waterloo himself, Wellington, was able to see the forces at work in England as "a revolution by due course of law." Revolution it must be, certainly; revolution that cannot stop short of democracy, of liberty and equality for all classes. Arnold's liberalism had become a kind of necessitarianism—and in the process it was transformed to something very different from what he defined as "the great middle-class liberalism, which had for the cardinal points of its belief the Reform Bill of 1832, and local self-government, in politics; in the social sphere, free-trade, unrestricted competition, and the making of large industrial fortunes; in the religious sphere, the Dissidence of Dissent and the Protestantism of the Protestant religion."[7]

What Arnold learned in the practice of his school inspectorship is what, in fact, distinguishes him from nearly all his contemporaries who wrote on politics and society.

Himself of the middle class, the son of an Anglican clergy-man, and brought up in those playgrounds of the aristocracy, Winchester, Rugby, and Oxford, he was making a constant round of visits to the schools and into the society of the lower middle class, the less wealthy of the Protestant Nonconformists. If the poorest classes in England never got to school at all, their homes and habitats were not so separated from the schools Arnold visited but that he could see them too in all their squalor. He found in himself a warm sympathy for the teachers who worked in these schools, but he also developed a keen sense of the disparity between the testimony of his eyes and the public utterances of the political liberals; "claptrap" became one of his characteristic words. Two memorable journeys to the Continent to visit schools as an agent of Royal Commissions in 1859 and 1865 served to show him as nothing else could have done the distinction between English chaos and the operation of modern ideas at their best, in France and Prussia.

From the date of the first of these foreign visits, in fact, it became impossible for him to avoid writing on social and political matters. When he prepared his long report on *The Popular Education of France* for publication, he prefixed to it an essay on "Democracy" that summed up much of the doctrine I have touched upon. His lectures as Professor of Poetry at Oxford, which began with some concepts of the "modern element" in past literatures that seem to have been suggested by his father's approach to the classics, slipped easily after the Continental journey into a discourse on Heinrich Heine as the spokesman of the "modern spirit" of revolution and liberalism; a lecture on "The Function of Criticism at the Present Time" is best remembered for holding up the claptrap of some self-satisfied politicians against the picture of a pathetic child-murder in the brutal conditions of the industrial slums, and the final lecture from the chair of poetry, "Culture and Its Enemies," was frankly political and social and became the first chapter of his best-known book, *Culture and Anarchy*.

Arnold's liberalism, then, rested on the double conviction that in the modern world democracy was inevitable and that it was the only condition compatible with human dignity. But the liberal ideal, in the hands of most Liberal politicians, was distorted by one of two forces—the strong bias of the Protestant Dissenters and the rigid systematizing of the doctrinaire Utilitarians. To the former Arnold gave the name "Mialism," to the latter "Millism," taking as his types the men who seemed to be the acknowledged leaders of the two groups.

Edward Miall was a man of great energy, who worked throughout a long life to secure the disestablishment of the Church of England and the separation of church and state. He was proprietor of the largest weekly newspaper of the dissenting groups, *The Nonconformist*, dedicated, as it proclaimed at the head of each issue, to "The Dissidence of Dissent and the Protestantism of the Protestant Religion." As a member of the Newcastle Commission, which sent Arnold to France to study elementary schools, Miall held firm against the majority of the Commissioners (and against Arnold's most heartfelt conviction) in his belief that government assistance to education was both superfluous and prejudicial.

Of the two terms, "Mialism" came first in Arnold's invention, in the Preface to *Culture and Anarchy*, written at the end of 1868. It was paired with "Millism" in the Preface to *St. Paul and Protestantism* in the spring of 1870 —and curiously enough, Arnold was rather proud of completing his pair. I say "curiously," because in fact Carlyle had been there before him, by a generation, alliteration and all. "The Millennarians have come forth on the right hand, and the Millites on the left," he wrote in "Signs of the Times" in 1829, with reference to John Stuart Mill's father James. "The Fifth-monarchy men prophesy from the Bible, and the Utilitarians from Bentham."[8]

The extent of Arnold's saturation in Carlyle (if I may digress for a moment) is hard to exaggerate, in the political as in the spiritual aspect of his writings. His terminology is Carlylean: his fondness for the German *Geist*, *Zeitgeist*, *Philistine* (no one of which he used precisely as Carlyle had used them, but no one of which was an attempt to escape its Carlylean associations), for the term "machinery" to characterize the age's concern for numbers and external organization rather than internal development; for the term "perfection" as an inward spiritual condition at which we must aim, for the term "culture" as the means to perfection. "Not for internal perfection," said Carlyle, "but for external combinations and arrangements, for institutions, constitutions,—for Mechanism of one sort or other, do [men today] hope and struggle. . . . The great law of culture is: Let each become all that he was created capable of being; expand, if possible, to his full growth. . . . A harmonious development of being [is] the first and last object of all true culture." "Culture . . . believes in perfection," said Arnold, "is the study and pursuit of perfection. . . . Culture . . . places human perfection in an *internal* condition, in the growth and predominance of our humanity proper, as distinguished from our animality. . . . Finally, perfection,—as culture from a thorough disinterested study of human nature and human experience learns to conceive it,—is a harmonious expansion of *all* the powers which make the beauty and worth of human nature."[9]

Whatever of transcendentalism there is in Arnold's view of the State is also an inheritance from Carlyle. For Arnold's State is not only the Burkeian "people themselves in their collective and corporate character," it is an idea that transcends material definition, and here we are in Carlyle's territory: "To understand man, . . . we must look beyond the individual man and his actions or interests, and view him in combination with his fellows. It is in Society that man first feels what he is; first becomes what he can be. In Society an altogether new set of spiritual activities are evolved in him, and the old immeasurably quickened and strengthened. Society is the genial element wherein his nature first lives and grows; the solitary man were but a small portion of himself, and must continue forever folded in, stunted and only half alive."[10]

Finally, Arnold learned a rhetorical method from Carlyle. His designation of the aristocracy as the Barbarians, of the middle class as the Philistines, imitates Carlyle's coinage of the terms "Dilettantism" and "Mammonism" for the same two classes in *Past and Present*. And he learned the rhetoric of ridicule. Carlyle turns up where you least expect him in Arnold—perhaps indeed where Arnold least expected him. You may remember the famous chapters in *Past and Present* on "Morrison's pill"— that universal cure-all manufactured by James Morison, who called himself "the Hygeist," to which Carlyle compared such Liberal machinery as the secret ballot. In "The Function of Criticism at the Present Time," Arnold speaks about the systematizing liberal theologians of his day, Bishop Colenso and Frances Power Cobbe: "[Their] works often have much ability; they often spring out of sincere convictions, and a sincere wish to do good; and they sometimes, perhaps, do good. Their fault is (if I may be permitted to say so) one which they have in common with the British College of Health, in the New Road. Every one knows the British College of Health; it is that building with the lion and the statue of the Goddess Hygeia before it; at least I am sure about the lion, though I am not absolutely certain about the Goddess Hygeia. This building does credit, perhaps, to the resources of Dr. Morison and his disciples; but it falls a good deal short of one's idea of what a British College of Health ought to be. In England, where we hate public interference and love individual enterprise, we have a whole crop of places like the British College of Health; the grand name without the grand thing."[11] The British College of Health, that is, was the name assumed by Dr. Morison for the factory that turned out his patent pills.

If there is so much of Carlyle in Arnold, is not Arnold ungrateful to criticize Carlyle so often as he does, and should he not acknowledge the debt? In the first place, as we saw last evening, he did acknowledge the debt, handsomely, in the lecture on Emerson; he did it also in the lecture on Heine.[12] To acknowledge a debt need not be to subordinate one's self to the creditor; scholars above all should learn that there can be a balance between generous acknowledgment of a predecessor and independence of mind, that partial disagreement need not be accompanied by total denunciation, or warm praise by total subscription. In the second place, and quite simply, Carlyle lacked the very qualities of balance and disinterestedness Arnold was most concerned to enforce; he did indeed have "for the functions of the critic, a little too much of the self-will and eccentricity of a genuine son of Great Britain." How else can one make clear the unintellectual climate in which English writers work than by showing the effect of that climate not merely on the hacks and minor writers—the Kinglakes, the Donaldsons, the Charles Forsters—but on the men of genius, the men most praised by their contemporaries, the Carlyles, the Macaulays, the Ruskins?[13] No one today would go to Carlyle for political wisdom; one would, I think, go to Arnold for that commodity.

To return to the Mialists, that is to the Protestant Dissenters who made up the great body of the Philistine middle class: the great objection to them, in Arnold's view, was their unthinking devotion to slogans and axioms which, when examined in the light of reason, proved either meaningless or, all too often, vicious. When the

Reverend Frederick James Jobson was elected president of the Wesleyan Conference in 1869, he knelt and prayed silently before the assembled delegates, then rose and addressed them: "We are resolved to continue firm in our adherence to Scriptural Protestantism, united in Christ with all evangelical churches, but never consenting to any alliance with the 'Man of Sin' "—with the Pope, the Roman Catholic church, that is. And what was the practical effect of this amiable statement? Jobson made it clear in the very next sentence—that the Roman Catholics in Ireland were to be prevented at all costs from gaining any part of the lands or income that now belonged to the Anglican Church of Ireland: "With those who advocate concurrent endowment or indiscriminate endowment, or who, though bound by oath to 'drive away damnable heresy,' can Judas-like betray the truth for pieces of silver, we can have no sympathy." The most popular preacher of the day, Charles Haddon Spurgeon, proclaimed to an audience of seven thousand in his Metropolitan Tabernacle, at a meeting presided over by the Liberal leader John Bright, that the Dissenters of England would rather leave the Anglican church undisturbed in Ireland than that "any share of the Church property should be given to the Papists."[14]

Some two years earlier, one William Murphy, who called himself the "agent of the London Protestant Electoral Union" (and no one seems quite to have known what that was), toured some of the industrial towns of the Midlands giving lectures. He demanded the use of the town hall in Birmingham; when it was denied him, a wooden "tabernacle" was erected for his use in the center of the city. There for nearly a week he addressed his audiences; on the platform with him one night was a member of Parliament; presiding were dissenting clergymen from the neighborhood, including a Methodist minister from Walsall named W. Cattle. And what was Murphy's message? "I say, then, away with the Mass! It is from the bottomless pit; and in the bottomless pit shall all liars have their part, in the lake that burneth with fire and brimstone." "When all the praties [potatoes] were black in Ireland, why didn't the priests say the hocus-pocus over them, and make them all good again?" "What I wish to say to you as Protestant husbands is, *Take care of your wives!*" "My object is to protect your wives and daughters. If Mayors and magistrates don't care for their wives and daughters, I do. I care for my wife, and therefore she shall not go to the confessional." And then his noble assertion of his right to free speech: "I will carry out my lectures if they walk over my body as a dead corpse; and I say to the Mayor of Birmingham that he is my servant while I am in Birmingham, and as my servant he must do his duty and protect me." When the member of Parliament who had appeared on the platform with him asked, in the House, for assurance that Murphy's rights would be protected, the Conservative Home Secretary, Gathorne Hardy, replied that though the lecturer's language was "only fit to be addressed to thieves or murderers," yet "I do not think he is to be deprived, I do not think that anything I have said could justify the inference that he is to be deprived, of the right of protection in a place built by him for the purpose of these lectures; because the language is not language which affords grounds for a criminal prosecution." "No," comments Arnold, "nor to be silenced by Mayor, or Home Secretary, or any administrative authority on earth, simply on their notion of what is discreet and reasonable! This is in perfect consonance with our public opinion, and with our national love for the assertion of personal liberty."[15]

Arnold has been severely criticized by modern scholars for suggesting that indeed Government *did* have some duty to stop Murphy. At this distance in time Murphy's speeches are remarkable only for their incredible bad taste; we cannot take them seriously, and are either uncomfortable at Arnold's taste in reprinting them or wonder what the fuss is about. Things looked quite different in those hot summer days in Birmingham, with its large population of imported Roman Catholic Irish laborers in competition for jobs with the native English population. Murphy's speeches touched off three days of rioting, brought under control only by the troops; houses and shops were burned, men were killed. One need not come from Detroit to Chicago in these days to paint the picture. With a writer like Arnold, so topical in his allusions, I sometimes think an editor has his use, merely in making clear just what was going on.

The great tasks of the Liberals were first, the settlement of the Irish question on terms that would give the Irish equality in the partnership with England, that would make the ties ties of mutual respect rather than patronage and force; and, second, the improvement of the lot of the industrial lower classes in England, through the franchise, to be sure, but also through education and through some intervention to protect their employment in off seasons and hard times. At every turn, in the Irish question and in the provision of public compulsory education, the Liberal government was thwarted by its fear of losing the support of the Nonconformist middle class. Sometimes, as when he handled the remarks of Murphy, or of Jobson, or of Spurgeon, Arnold's irony against the Nonconformists was bitter. Sometimes it was more genial.

The political Dissenters of course aimed at the root of the Establishment with their efforts to secure a complete separation of Church and State, but this was obviously a hopeless campaign; meanwhile they might succeed in lopping off some of the lesser evidences of the tyranny of the Establishment. Some of their victories were notable and significant—the abolition of compulsory church rates, the opening of the ancient universities to Nonconformists. Other campaigns were somewhat more trifling. One of these was the bill several times introduced by a private member of Parliament to permit the marriage of a man to his deceased wife's sister. Such a marriage was prohibited by canon law in the Church of England as being within the forbidden degrees and hence incestuous; it became a statutory prohibition only by an Act of Parliament early in the nineteenth century. Inasmuch as the Protestant Dissenters had no religious scruples against such marriages, the law became to them one more symbol of the imposition by the government of the principles of the Established Church. A Dissenter who wished to marry his deceased wife's sister might always, of course, go abroad and have the ceremony performed in countries which imposed no barrier, but this was expensive. The number of such marriages over the years can hardly have been very large and the issue seems rather trifling in the great scheme of things (Parliament itself took the view that it had more important matters to concern itself with), but the campaign was persistent. On the night of April 21, 1869, John Bright took his seat in the House without having consulted the calendar for the evening, and discovered a debate in progress on the question. As the most eloquent spokesman for Liberalism and Dissent, he could not remain silent: "The Church of England permits the marriage of first cousins. . . . Is there any man of common-sense who will not say that on every natural ground the marriage of first cousins is more objectionable than the marriage of a man with his deceased wife's sister? . . . I have always thought the consideration of the position of children by these marriages one of immense importance. . . . It is notorious beyond dispute that there are many cases . . . in which the dying mother hopes that her sister may become in a closer sense than that of aunt the protector of her children. I appeal to . . . all . . . opponents of the Bill, as to whether they themselves deem the man who marries his deceased wife's sister a profligate man? ('No.') . . . Is there any man that regards a woman married to her deceased sister's husband as an immoral person who is not to be admitted to his house, and who he thinks would be likely to taint the society of his wife and daughters? (Hear, hear.) No such feeling exists. (Hear, hear.) And if there are children of those marriages, there is no man in this House or out of it cruel enough—I nearly used a harsher word—to point to those children by the almost odious name of bastard. (Cheers.)" The speech needed very little alteration at Arnold's hand. Leo, the young reporter for the *Daily Telegraph*, attending at the deathbed of the wife of the wealthy industrialist Bottles, Esq., sees there Mrs. Bottles' maiden sister Hannah, and, somewhat more interesting, a lovely niece named Mary Jane. He speculates that if the bill before Parliament should become law, Miss Hannah will become the next Mrs. Bottles, since everybody wishes it that way. "Everybody but old Bottles himself, I should think," retorts the cynical foreign correspondent who is also there. "Don't envy him at all!—shouldn't so much mind if it were the younger one, though."

"These light words of my friend," young Leo writes, "seemed to touch a spring in me. Instantly I felt myself visited by a shower of ideas, full of import for the Liberal party and for the future. . . . 'And why not the younger one, Nick?' said I gently: 'why not? Either as a successor to Miss Hannah or in lieu of Miss Hannah, why not? Let us apply John Bright's crucial tests. Is she his first cousin? Could there be a more natural companion for Selina and the other Bottles girls? Or,—to take the moral ground so touchingly and irresistibly chosen by our great popular tribune,—if legislation on this subject were impeded by the party of bigotry, if they chose not to wait for it, if they got married without it, and if you were to meet them on the boulevard at Paris during their wedding tour, should you go up to Bottles and say: Mr. Bottles, you are a profligate man?' 'Oh, dear, no,' said Nick; 'I should never dream of it.' 'And if you met them a year later on the same spot,' I continued, 'with a Normandy nurse behind them carrying a baby, should you cry out to the poor little thing: Bastard?' 'Nothing of the kind,' he answered."[16]

The Protestant Dissenters rallied round what they called Scriptural Christianity, or the Gospel Feast, and judged all things from that single point of view.[17] They inpinged most strongly upon Arnold's professional career in their insistence upon what was called "voluntaryism" in education. Neither the sects nor the Establishment was inclined to give up religious instruction in the schools, and while the Establishment might reasonably expect that state-supported schools would give religious instruction an Anglican tinge the Dissenters saw public education as a threat to their doctrinal control of their children. They therefore insisted that schools be set up and controlled by the sects or by private persons, and one large group of Dissenters, the Congregationalists, for some years declined to accept Parliamentary grants in aid of their schools rather than submit to the concomitant inspection by Arnold and his colleagues. Bitter experience in time told them that their operation would founder without state support, but they retained their prejudices, and even the great Education Act of 1870, designed and carried through Parliament by Arnold's brother-in-law W. E. Forster, made far greater concessions to voluntaryism than Arnold would have wished.

The Utilitarians, or philosophical radicals, arrived at much the same point from quite a different direction. Their opposition to an established church sprang, theoretically at least, from a rationalist, non-Christian philosophy; their support of voluntaryism in education, from a fear of public education as an instrument to enforce the power of government over the individual. And they too were by no means behindhand in seeing the force of Arnold's writings as against their own principles. A witty article in the *Saturday Review*, anonymous but by Fitzjames Stephen, early accused Arnold of being obsessed by "the transcendental theory of philosophy" and therefore unable to grasp the impeccable reasoning which governed English Liberal policy. "In fact," wrote Stephen, "no nation in the world is so logical as the English nation. . . . Once get it well convinced of the truth of a general principle, . . . and it will do anything. For instance, the English nation believes in political economy, and the consequence is that it is the only nation in the world which has established free trade. . . . Bentham persuaded the English nation that the greatest happiness of the greatest number was the true rule for legislation, and every part of the law has been reformed by degrees by the application, more or less skillful and complete, of that abstract principle."[18] When Arnold set out to reply to this assertion, he adopted as his motto a few sentences from Burke: "Our antagonist is our helper. This amicable conflict with difficulty obliges us to an intimate acquaintance with our object, and compels us to consider it in all its relations. It will not suffer us to be superficial."[19]

The warfare against the Benthamites had rallied to the battle cry of Carlyle for more than a generation—against those who "assure us that 'the greatest-happiness principle' is to make a heaven of earth" in an instant, "Liberals, Economists, Utilitarians," Radicals, "or whatsoever they are called," the modern mechanists or scholasticists who, after a brief life on the Continent, were now dead everywhere except in England. "Consider the old Schoolmen," said Carlyle, "and their pilgrimage towards Truth: the faithfulest endeavour, incessant unwearied motion, often great natural vigour; only no progress: nothing but antic feats of one limb poised against the other; there they balanced, somersetted, and made postures. . . . So it is, so will it always be, with all System-makers and builders of logical card-castles; of which class a certain remnant must, in every age, as they do in our own, survive and build."[20] Arnold thus addressed his final Oxford audience: "After hearing Bentham cried loudly up as the renovator of modern society, and Bentham's mind and ideas proposed as the rulers of our future, I open the *Deontology*. There I read: 'While Xenophon was writing his history and Euclid teaching geometry, Socrates and Plato were talking nonsense under pretence of teaching wisdom and morality. This morality of theirs consisted in words; this wisdom of theirs was the denial of matters known to every man's experience.' From the moment of reading that, I am delivered from the bondage of Bentham! the fanaticism of his adherents can touch me no longer. I feel the inadequacy of his mind and ideas for supplying the rule of human society, for perfection. Culture tends always thus to deal with the men of a system, of disciples, of a school; with men like Comte, or the late Mr. Buckle, or Mr. Mill. However much it may find to admire in these personages, or in some of them, it nevertheless remembers the text: 'Be not ye called Rabbi!' and it soon passes on from any Rabbi."[21]

Though in many respects the doctrines of the Benthamites sound more modern to us than the doctrines of a Carlyle or a Ruskin—and Arnold was perfectly aware of the extent to which they were in the main current of modern advance—they were not without their ridiculous side. There was Comte's "religion of humanity," which had its active followers in Arnold's friend and fellow-Rugbeian Richard Congreve and in Frederic Harrison, the brilliant young controversialist to whose ridicule of "the man of culture" we owe *Culture and Anarchy*. There was Bentham's wish that he might come to life once every hundred years to see the increase in human happiness as his principles were applied, and his bequest of his body to University College, London, so that, dressed in his clothes and with his favorite walking stick at his knee, his skeleton might perpetually preside over the rational nonsectarian institution he had founded—and there, of course, Bentham may be seen to this day. Irrational weaknesses of this sort in the great rationalists of the day were easily vulnerable to Arnold's ridicule; he needed only to quote from Congreve's translation of Comte's *Catechism of Positive Religion* to disclose its silliness, and his playful irony leaves Bentham's skeleton just a little more naked, when he speaks of the nervousness of a London jeweler as his commuter train passes near a spot where, only a few days earlier, another jeweler had been brutally murdered and robbed: "What I took for the ignoble clinging to life of a comfortable worldling, was, perhaps, only the ardent longing of a faithful Benthamite, traversing an age still dimmed by the last mists of transcendentalism, to be spared long enough to see his religion in the full and final blaze of its triumph. This respectable man, whom I imagined to be going up to London to serve his shop, or to buy shares, or to attend an Exeter Hall meeting, or to assist at the deliberations of the Marylebone Vestry, was even, perhaps, in real truth, on a pious pilgrimage, to obtain from Mr. Bentham's executors a sacred bone of his great, dissected master." [22]

Inevitably the Benthamites, like any other party, had to rally round slogans and catchwords. Phrases that might in John Stuart Mill be a part of a reasoned argument became, in the mouths of his followers, ends in themselves. Mill conceived that the principle of liberty embraced liberty of conscience, of thought and feeling, of public expression; it embraced also "liberty of tastes and pursuits; of framing the plan of our life to suit our own character; of doing as we like, subject to such consequences as may follow." [23] In *Culture and Anarchy*, that chapter which sets forth most clearly Arnold's central conception of the State is headed, somewhat ironically, "Doing as One Likes"; and the essence of his reply to the Benthamite slogan-mongers was that doing as one likes is not in itself a virtue, but is a virtue only if what one likes is in fact virtuous. "The great thing, it will be observed, is to find our *best* self, and to seek to affirm nothing but that; not,—as we English with our over-value for merely being free and busy have been so accustomed to do,—resting satisfied with a self which comes uppermost long before our best self, and affirming that with blind energy." In short, let us heed the instruction of Bishop Wilson in both its parts: "Firstly, never go against the best light you have; secondly, take care that your light be not darkness."[24]

With the economics of free trade Arnold had little sympathy. As early as 1848 he described its slogans as "twaddle."[25] Twenty years later his hardest-hitting attack on the Liberals in *Culture and Anarchy* was directed at the mechanical application of their doctrine of free trade, supported by the confused sentimentality of well-meaning do-gooders. "I remember, only the other day, a good man looking with me upon a multitude of children who were gathered before us in one of the most miserable regions of London,—children eaten up with disease; half-sized, half-fed, half-clothed, neglected by their parents, without health, without home, without hope,—said to me: 'The one thing really needful is to teach these little ones to succour one another, if only with a cup of cold water; but now, from one end of the country to the other, one hears nothing but the cry for knowledge, knowledge, knowledge!' And yet surely, so long as these children are there in these festering masses, without health, without home, without hope, and so long as their multitude is perpetually swelling, charged with misery they must still be for themselves, charged with misery they must still be for us, whether they help one another with a cup of cold water or no; and the knowledge how to prevent their accumulating is necessary, even to give their moral life and growth a fair chance! . . . [Have not the self-satisfied middle-class defenders of *laissez-faire*] to learn that if they call their private acquaintances imprudent or unlucky, when, with no means of support for them or with precarious means, they have a large family of children, then they ought not to call the State well managed and

49

prosperous merely because its manufactures and its citizens multiply, if the manufactures, which bring new citizens into existence just as much as if they had actually begotten them, bring more of them into existence than they can maintain, or are too precarious to go on maintaining those whom for a while they maintained?"[26]

Free trade, like political Dissent, came home to Arnold's professional concern when the responsible head of his department, Robert Lowe, in 1861–62 proposed to bring education into accord with the principles of supply and demand by means of a new scheme of "payment by results," in which grants to schools were based entirely on the number of pupils who, having attended a certain minimum number of days, should pass satisfactorily examinations in reading, writing, and arithmetic given by the state's inspectors. The proposal was based, as we shall see, on doctrines not unlike those of Mill in his essay *On Liberty*, and though widespread opposition, in which Arnold's own pen was employed, led to some modification, "payment by results" remained an effective conception in the administration of the educational funds for the rest of Arnold's life and longer, and his inspectoral chores, therefore, included examining the pupils in the schools he visited in those three elementary skills.[27]

For the Mialists Arnold sometimes expressed admiration on grounds of character, never thought; for the leading Liberal intellectuals of his day his regard was a good deal higher than for the run-of-the-mill political Dissenter: Fitzjames Stephen, John Morley, Frederic Harrison might have every assurance that Arnold's handling of their doctrines, even his bantering them, was a mark of his respect. Of John Stuart Mill, the acknowledged leader of his generation of Utilitarians, Arnold always spoke in very nearly the highest terms. Mill, of course, was more than sixteen years older than Arnold, and the greater part of his work was done before Arnold entered the field of political and social discussion, though to be sure the decade of the sixties was the height of the Liberal party's deference to the intellectual image of Mill, which culminated in Mill's two-year term in Parliament. (There is something a little comic in Hansard's accounts of bows in Mill's direction as the members on both sides of the House took occasion in the course of parliamentary debate to pay tribute to his great mind.)

Arnold had known Mill's writings at least since he was obliged to study the first two books of the *Logic* in preparation for the Oriel fellowship examination in 1845.[28] His earliest public reference to him was at the beginning of the essay on Marcus Aurelius in November, 1863, when he alluded to Mill's sensitivity to the emotional and the dynamic, as well as to the intellectual impact of Christianity. "It is because Mr. Mill has attained to the perception of truths of this nature, that he is,—instead of being, like the school from which he proceeds, doomed to sterility,—a writer of distinguished mark and influence, a writer deserving all attention and respect; it is (I must be pardoned for saying) because he is not sufficiently leavened with them, that he falls just short of being a great writer."[29] *Schools and Universities on the Continent* in 1868 twice mentions in very high terms Mill's reflections on the substance of English education. But having in the final Oxford lecture taken Mill (understandably) as the great teacher to whose doctrine the modern Utilitarians, rightly or wrongly, subscribed, he soon coined, as we have seen, the term "Millism" to represent that doctrine, especially as it degenerated in the hands of the followers.[30] He repeated the term "Millism" in *Friendship's Garland* (1871), but when he wrote a Preface for *Higher Schools and Universities in Germany* in 1874, the year after Mill's death, he declared his wish to abandon it: "The principle that the State should have nothing to do with religion depends on . . . propositions advanced respectively by those two powers in this country which we have elsewhere called Millism and Miallism. These nicknames give offence, and we will not employ them here; one of them, besides, might turn out to be not strictly accurate. For Mr. Mill, who was not, perhaps, the great spirit that some of his admirers suppose, but who was a singularly acute, ardent, and interesting man, was capable of following lights that led him away from the regular doctrine of philosophical radicalism, and on no question was he more capable of doing this than in one where the Catholics of Ireland were concerned. We will say then, instead of Millism and Miallism, Secularist Radicalism and Nonconformity. Both call themselves Liberal."[31] Speaking at the opening of the session of University College, Liverpool, in 1882, Arnold described the impact of modern thought upon England after the long severance from the Continent in the wars against France: "The Continent was reopened, the century advanced, time and experience brought their lessons, lovers of free and clear thought such as the late Mr. John Stuart Mill arose amongst us; but one could not say that they have by any means founded among us the reign of lucidity."[32] And perhaps Arnold's last word on Mill—still, be it noted, filled with the sense of Mill's grasping the temper of the modern spirit and the current of the modern intellect—was published less than two years before his own death: "A Liberal leader . . . should see clearly how the world is going, what our modern tendencies and needs really are, and what is routine and fiction in that which we have inherited from the past. But of how few men of Mr. Gladstone's age can it be said that they see this! Certainly not of Mr. Gladstone. Some of whom it cannot be said may be more interesting figures than those of whom it can; Cardinal Newman is a more interesting figure, Mr. Gladstone himself is a more interesting figure, than John Stuart Mill. But a Liberal leader of whom it cannot be said that he sees how the world is really going is in a false situation."[33]

Arnold's debate with Mill, then, is always within the framework of intellectual respect. But both Mill and his disciples appear to Arnold to lack the flexibility Arnold himself valued so highly; all too often theirs was a dogmatism untempered by experience, incapable even of self-criticism. It is striking how frequently Mill's essay *On Liberty* seems to be in Arnold's mind as he turns his attention to political and social matters—how often, even when he does not mention it, he seems to be amplifying or answering it. The essay appeared in 1859, just as Arnold was making his first journey to study the schools of the Continent, and he wrote to his mother from Strasbourg: "It is worth reading attentively, being one of the few books that inculcate tolerance in an unalarming and inoffensive way."[34] It provided, as we have seen, the opening, or text, for Arnold's essay on Marcus Aurelius four years later. Arnold perfectly agreed with Mill that the ideals of the modern world must draw from a much wider range of sources than the Bible alone, and it is no doubt this shared conviction which leads to his praise of Mill for a spiritual insight greater than that of many of his followers. Marcus Aurelius, however, figured in the essay *On Liberty* as a crowning instance of a very good, wise and great man who carried his conviction of his own rightness to the point of persecution—persecution of a religion which the modern world is convinced is right and which suffered irreparably from that very persecution: "To my mind," wrote Mill, "this is one of the most tragical facts in all history. It is a bitter thought, how different a thing the Christianity of the world might have been, if the Christian faith had been adopted as the religion of the empire under the auspices of Marcus Aurelius instead of those of Constantine."[35] Arnold treats the question from the same point of view as Mill, even with almost the same rhetoric. "Who will venture to affirm that, by the alliance of Christianity with the virtue and intelligence of men like the Antonines,—of the best product of Greek and Roman civilisation, while Greek and Roman civilisation had yet life and power,—Christianity and the world, as well as the Antonines themselves, would not have been the gainers? That alliance was not to be. The Antonines lived and died with an utter misconception of Christianity; Christianity grew up in the Catacombs, not on the Palatine."[36] Arnold and Mill exonerate Marcus Aurelius on much the same ground: that Christianity necessarily appeared to him very different from what it appears to us. "As a ruler of mankind, he deemed it his duty not to suffer society to fall in pieces; and saw not how, if its existing ties were removed, any others could be formed which could again knit it together. The new religion openly aimed at dissolving these ties; unless, therefore, it was his duty to adopt that religion, it seemed to be his duty to put it down." So says Mill; Arnold, here as almost always, looks from the general to the particular, from the historical to the modern, and as he does so, shows a certain spirit of mischief. "The Christianity which [the Antonines] aimed at repressing was, in their conception of it, something philosophically contemptible, politically subversive, and morally abominable. As men, they sincerely regarded it much as well-conditioned people, with us, regard Mormonism; as rulers, they regarded it much as Liberal statesmen, with us, regard the Jesuits. A kind of Mormonism, constituted as a vast secret society, with obscure aims of political and social subversion, was what Antoninus Pius and Marcus Aurelius believed themselves to be repressing when they punished Christians. . . . [And] who can doubt that among the professing Christians of the second century, as among the professing Christians of the nineteenth, there was plenty of folly, plenty of rabid nonsense, plenty of gross fanaticism?"[37] The mischief, of course, lies not only in the flick at Christians both inside and outside the Establishment. It has its eye on the inconsistency between the characteristic Liberal condemnation of the Jesuits—typified, for example, by Macaulay's insane rhetoric in the *History of England*—and Mill's rather fatuous and overblown rhetoric in defense of Mormonism, a religious and social phenomenon which, for Arnold, was supremely unimportant in the main course of human events.[38]

Again and again Arnold's wit plays lightly where Mill's humorlessness weighs him down. "I acknowledge that the tendency of all opinions to become sectarian is not cured by the freest discussion, but is often heightened and exacerbated thereby; the truth which ought to have been, but was not, seen, being rejected all the more violently because proclaimed by persons regarded as opponents," says Mill. Here is Arnold's handling of the idea: "I remember a Nonconformist manufacturer, in a town of the Midland counties, telling me that when he first came there, some years ago, the place had no Dissenters; but he had opened an Independent chapel in it, and now Church and Dissent were pretty equally divided, with sharp contests between them. I said that this seemed a pity. 'A pity?' cried he; 'not at all! Only think of all the zeal and activity which the collision calls forth!' 'Ah, but, my dear friend,' I answered, 'only think of all the nonsense which you now hold quite firmly, which you would never have held if you had not been contradicting your adversary in it all these years!' "[39]

If Arnold were only rhetorically superior, his distinction from Mill would not much interest us. His wit, indeed, all too often misfired in his own day and offends—or perhaps more often escapes—a good many of his readers today. But the man who looks at the particular will avoid some kinds of mistakes. Take the single example of Mill's program for education in the final chapter of the essay *On Liberty*. "Is it not almost a self-evident axiom, that the State should require and compel the education, up to a certain standard, of every human being who is born its citizen? . . . Hardly any one indeed will deny that it is one of the most sacred duties of the parents, . . . after summoning a human being into the world, to give to that being an education fitting him to perform his part well in life towards others and towards himself." Arnold would have agreed with his whole heart. But what are Mill's conclusions? That the government should leave education in private hands, but should pay part or all the fees of the neediest children; that it should make education compulsory, however, should examine publicly all the children from an early age, and should reexamine them annually "with a gradually extending range of subjects, so as to make the universal acquisition, and what is more, retention, of a certain minimum of general knowledge, virtually compulsory"; that the father of a child that does not come up to the standard for its age be fined and the child "put to school at his expense." "A general State education is a mere contrivance for moulding people to be exactly like one another," he affirmed.

It is hard to know where to begin here—whether with the notion that a state examination is less prescriptive than a state education, or with the practical cruelty, as Arnold saw it, of making all hinge upon a single annual examination, even for very small children, or with the principle of preserving the father's freedom to neglect the child, and only punishing him after the damage has been done.[40] As for freedom of choice, diversity of education, and the voluntary principle, Arnold saw all these things at work in England—and this is how they looked to him. Having given an account of the schools established by the Crown in North Germany, he goes on: "In England how different is the part which in this matter our governors are accustomed to play! The Licensed Victuallers" (and let me remind you that licensed victuallers in English terminology are keepers of public houses, or taverns and bars) "or the Commercial Travellers propose to make a school for their children; and I suppose, in the matter of schools, one may call the Licensed Victuallers or the Commercial

Travellers ordinary men, with their natural taste for the bathos still strong; and a Sovereign with the advice of men like Wilhelm von Humboldt or Schleiermacher may, in this matter, be a better judge, and nearer to right reason. And it will be allowed, probably, that right reason would suggest that, to have a sheer school of Licensed Victuallers' children, or a sheer school of Commercial Travellers' children, and to bring them all up, not only at home but at school too, in a kind of odour of licensed victualism or of bagmanism, is not a wise training to give to these children. . . . But, in England, the action of the national guides or governors is, for a Royal Prince or a great Minister to go down to the opening of the Licensed Victuallers' or of the Commercial Travellers' school, to take the chair, to extol the energy and self-reliance of the Licensed Victuallers or the Commercial Travellers, to be all of their way of thinking, to predict full success to their schools, and never so much as to hint to them that they are probably doing a very foolish thing, and that the right way to go to work with their children's education is quite different."[41]

The heart of the difference between Mill and Arnold rests, it seems to me, in the conception of the State. For Arnold, as we have seen, the State was an aspect of the people in it, and this, I submit, is a great deal closer to the fact than the anonymous, faceless, monolithic conception that haunts Mill. Mill fusses with instances in which "the thing to be done is likely to be better done by individuals than by the government," or in which "individuals may not do the particular thing so well, on the average, as the officers of government, [but in which] it is nevertheless desirable that it should be done by them, rather than by the government, as a means to their own mental education."[42] But whatever is done is done by people; if bridges are built, they are built by engineers; if the sick are healed, they are healed by doctors; if pupils are taught, they are taught by teachers. And the engineers, the doctors, the teachers, will have the same training and the same skills whether they are employed by the State or by what we now call "the private sector." Unless, of course, Mill meant—what it is nonsense to suppose he meant—to endorse the principle of self-education Arnold once described: "A man without the requisite scientific knowledge undertakes to build a difficult bridge; he builds three which tumble down, and so learns how to build a fourth which stands."[43] To be sure, Arnold himself was an agent of government. Nevertheless, Mill's distinction between what is done by government and by private enterprise is not a distinction between "government" and "the individual" but between one kind of management or administration and another—and even there the effect is not always what he fancies it to be.

Arnold's conception allowed also for something Mill left too little room for—disinterested devotion to a public ideal. When Arnold alluded to the State as the "collective best self," he meant to say that a man who is in a public position performs his tasks with a strong sense that he must do better than if he were merely working for himself. And it is here, I think, that we are perpetually being surprised by experience—at the sight of the politician, that is, who turns out to be seeking little for himself and much for the good of mankind.

Part of Arnold's respect for Mill arose from his conviction that Mill betrayed at every turn an idealism entirely out of keeping with the apparently rational and mechanical rigor of his writings. And this is doubtless the reason why, whenever Arnold ridiculed the Utilitarians, he chose the disciples of Mill rather than the leader himself. In the Preface to *Essays in Criticism* (1865), Arnold had said: "I have never been able to hit it off happily with the logicians. . . . They imagine truth something to be proved, I something to be seen; they something to be manufactured, I as something to be found. I have a profound respect for intuitions, and a very lukewarm respect for the elaborate machine-work of my friends the logicians. I have always thought that all which was worth much in this elaborate machine-work of theirs came from an intuition, to which they gave a grand name of their own. How did they come by this intuition? Ah! if they could tell us that."[44] He read Mill's *Autobiography* as soon as it appeared, and jotted down the telltale sentence in which Mill remarked that his wife "had at first reached her opinions by the moral intuition of a character of strong feeling."[45] Carlyle's initial exclamation that in Mill he had found "a new mystic" would not have been entirely confuted by the essay *On Liberty*.[46] In very many respects, Arnold and Mill were of the same mind. Moreover, Mill's formulation of abstract principles can still bring a wholesome check to our impulses; it is a great corrective for us to recall his remarks on the tyranny of public opinion before we judge our fellowmen.

But Mill was limited by his age more than he knew. He conceived of human progress as linear, all in the direction of Western Europe and England in the nineteenth century; other ways of life were merely inferior or infantile. He thought of man as essentially a rational creature; the effect of propaganda, of "the big lie," was beyond his ken. Social and economic forces he seldom judged correctly, and therefore tended to think that man's freedom was best ensured by the removal of controls, whereas often man's poverty and degradation, not man's freedom, come from an uncontrolled economy. The great revolutionary was in many ways a Liberal of the Past. Arnold, though he held many of Mill's convictions, came closer—as we see in his books on education, and more concisely in the hard-hitting attack on laissez-faire economy at the close of *Culture and Anarchy*—to being what he designated himself, "a Liberal of the Future."

III

JOY WHOSE GROUNDS ARE TRUE

John Stuart Mill once remarked that he was "one of the very few examples, in this country, of one who has, not thrown off religious belief, but never had it: I grew up in a negative state with regard to it."[1] It was a statement Arnold could never have made, and never would have wanted to make; but the state in which he grew up with regard to religion is often, I think, unwittingly misrepresented. The son of a clergyman *ought*, of course, to have been brought up in an atmosphere of piety and unquestioned literal adherence to creeds and dogmas from which, if he has any spirit in him, he *ought* to revolt. And therefore much has been made of the spiritual crisis Arnold is assumed to have undergone, by those whose picture of his home life is altogether too much that of Tennyson's "Supposed Confessions of a Second-Rate Sensitive Mind," with its simple piety learned at a mother's knee. So far as our admittedly scant evidence goes, this view of the matter is not borne out; without being paradoxical, I submit that Arnold never lost his faith, and that precisely for that reason he became a sounder spiritual guide than almost any of his contemporaries.

To say this is not, of course, to say that his conception of Christianity never changed during his formative years; but of what intelligent man, for whom religious matters are a central concern of life, can that not be said? The *Apologia pro vita sua* itself is a "History of My Religious Opinions," as Newman called it, up to the age of forty-four.

In no respect do Arnold and Mill differ more widely than in their relation to Christianity and to the Church, and nowhere, it seems to me, does Mill write with less ease, with more discomfort, than when he deals with these matters. For Mill's public morality is as conventional as anyone's could be, and though he was convinced that religion was both an unnecessary and an unsatisfactory base for morality he found himself in a society in which the conventional morality was apparently inextricably bound up with Christianity. And thus, when Arnold noted the inconsistency in Mill's *Autobiography* between the proposition that religion was the greatest enemy of morality and the statement a few pages later that in English society there was no high and noble standard of conduct "except among a few of the stricter religionists," he commented, "The little that *is* done for morality is done, then, by morality's greatest enemy!"[2] Another instance of Mill's uncertainty in dealing with Christianity—an instance which I hope is not niggling—is that in the very essay *On Liberty* in which he regards "utility" (that is, self-interest) "as the ultimate appeal on all ethical questions," he finds Christian morality inferior to pagan because by holding out the hope of heaven and the threat of hell it gives "to human morality an essentially selfish character, by disconnecting each man's feelings of duty from the interests of his fellow-creatures, except so far as self-interested inducement is offered to him for consulting them."[3] Much of this discomfort comes, surely, from Mill's education at the hands of a secular rationalist who conveyed to him an entirely exterior view of Christianity—and perhaps not even a rationally complete one.

Arnold, on the other hand, is as much at ease in Christianity, one is almost inclined to say, as the Pope himself. The son of a clergyman, he was entirely educated by clerics; both in the public schools and at Oxford, all the teachers (with negligible exceptions) were in orders. Had Arnold's father been a different sort of man—had he, indeed, been the sort of man popular prejudice paints him—or had Matthew Arnold been of a different disposition, rebellion—or a confusion like Clough's—would not have been surprising. As it was, his rebellion confined itself to a rather outrageous record of cutting services in the college chapel—and I think experience shows that a young man may cut chapel without being an atheist or a freethinker.[4] And of course there was his decision not to take holy orders—for, as we have seen, his competing for the Oriel fellowship carries the implication that he was at least open to the idea of a career in teaching that would have required ordination.

Dr. Arnold, in fact, had sensed clearly the difficulties of Christianity in the modern age—its conflict with the evidence of history and science as regards such matters as the inspiration of Scripture, the truth of prophecy, and miracles. Dr. Arnold was no systematic theologian, and the greater part of his doctrine was embodied in sermons preached in the chapel of Rugby School. The question of the inspiration of Scripture he dismissed as irrelevant to the real value of the Bible; and "it is only the *inspiration* of the books of the Scripture, and not their general *truth*, . . . that is, or can be, affected by the great majority of objections, critical, scientific, historical, and chronological, which have been brought at different times against various parts of the Bible. . . . Our Christian faith . . . has been totally unconcerned in the dispute."[5] Prophecy, in his view, was not the anticipation of history, and therefore the disproof of its evidence in no way affected the validity of the Bible. Miracles he inclined to judge on probability; he was firmly convinced of the miracle of Christ's resurrection, and if that be true, the truth of other particular miracles was of no great consequence. (In this respect, of course, his son came to differ from him.) Dr. Arnold used the very language of science to enforce his notion that the teachings of Christ, as moral rather than theological doctrine, retained their value unaltered: he spoke, as did Coleridge, of "an experimental knowledge" of their power; "experimental" was one of Matthew Arnold's favorite words in *Literature and Dogma*. Dr. Arnold recognized the danger in man's applying his notions of human personality to his idea of God and cautioned against the tendency to anthropomorphize God.

These sermons, which his son heard and in the atmosphere of which he was brought up, remained in his maturity "the most delightful and the most satisfactory to read, of all [my father's] writings."[6] And therefore Matthew Arnold went to Oxford with a faith quite different from the popular conception of Christianity. At the scholars' table at Balliol, "he used to say that the strict imposition of creeds had done more to break up than to unite churches, and nations, and families, and . . . he was the apostle of religious toleration in every direction."[7]

In an era when the higher criticism from Germany, especially in its destructive aspects, was shaking many young men, Matthew Arnold was unshaken because he was unsurprised; his father had made him acquainted with theological trends in Germany and had guided him in the criteria for judging what was fruitful and what was not. His father's friends, the lively group of religious intellectuals at Oriel whom Newman described in the *Apologia* with respect even while he disapproved their doctrines, gave Matthew Arnold a method of approach to the study of the Bible. But Spinoza was his great teacher. When he came to know Spinoza is uncertain: the earliest mention in his correspondence is a letter to Clough in October, 1850, in which he speaks of the philosopher's "positive and vivifying atmosphere" and adds, "I have been studying [him] lately with profit." That is almost certainly too late a date for first acquaintance. We know that his younger brother Thomas took a volume of Spinoza to New Zealand with him three years earlier, and the same brother later recalled that Strauss's *Life of Jesus* (published in English translation in 1846) left Matthew unaffected because all that was revolutionary in it he already knew from Spinoza.[8] A good many years later Arnold himself wrote: "It makes me rather angry to be affiliated to German Biblical critics; I have had to read masses of them, and they would have drowned me if it had not been for the corks I had brought from the study of Spinoza. To him I owe more than I can say."[9]

Spinoza was better known by name than in substance in England; Coleridge in the *Biographia Literaria* protests that he was commonly regarded as an atheist, and as late as 1861 he was denounced by a preacher in Canterbury Cathedral as an "atheistical Jew." His essay on the interpretation of the Bible, the *Tractatus Theologico-Politicus*, was not translated into English until 1862.[10] The German theologians, of course, recognized their debt to Spinoza; Schleiermacher, whom both Dr. Arnold and Matthew Arnold regarded very highly, pays him handsome tribute. I have pointed out that Arnold came to Spinoza and Goethe at about the same time, and it was the Spinozistic naturalism that most impressed him about Goethe:

> *For he pursued a lonely road,*
> *His eyes on Nature's plan;*
> *Neither made man too much a God,*
> *Nor God too much a man.*[11]

The key or central conception of Spinoza's metaphysics is that there can be no distinction between the creator and the created; the terms "God" and "Nature" are then identical, and Nature is infinite: there is no cause outside of Nature. His is a remarkably unified system, of which the logic appeared to him utterly compelling once we get rid of our common association of the notion of "God" with anthropomorphic and personal images. To call his system "atheistic" is as meaningless as to call it "pantheistic." [12] The great step Arnold took beyond his father was the acceptance of this concept as the point of view from which Christianity must be regarded in the modern world.

When Spinoza turned to the interpretation of the Judaeo-Christian Scripture, however, he did not use his philosophical conception as his starting point. His method, valid within any philosophical or religious system, was to read Scripture with regard to the claims Scripture actually makes for itself. "As to what God, or the Exemplar of the true life, may be, whether fire, or spirit, or light, or thought, or what not, this, I say, has nothing to do with faith any more than has the question how He comes to be Exemplar of the true life, whether it be because He has a just and merciful mind, or because all things exist and act through Him, and consequently that we understand through Him, and through Him see what is truly just and good. Everyone may think on such questions as he likes. Furthermore, faith is not affected, whether we hold that God is omnipresent essentially or potentially, . . . that He dictates laws like a prince, or that He sets them forth as eternal truths; that man obeys Him by virtue of free will, or by virtue of the necessity of the Divine decree; lastly, that the reward of the good and the punishment of the wicked is natural or supernatural; these and such like questions have no bearing on faith. . . . I will go further, and maintain that every man is bound to adapt these dogmas to his own way of thinking, and to interpret them according as he feels that he can give them his fullest and most unhesitating assent, so that he may the more easily obey God with his whole heart." And finally, he asserts that "between faith or theology, and philosophy, there is

no connection, nor affinity. . . . Philosophy has no end in
view save truth: faith, as we have abundantly proved,
looks for nothing but obedience and piety."[13] In his own
writings on Scripture, Arnold again and again suggests a
language that may be acceptable to modern patterns of
thought, but surprises us by admiring religious writers,
canonical or otherwise, who use quite a different language; Newman praised Arnold's "sympathy for what
[he did] not believe."[14] For Arnold, it is the moral intuition that counts, and the language in which it is conveyed
is unacceptable only when it becomes factious with respect to the metaphysical truth of its assertions. The
method is Spinoza's.

Spinoza handles many of the questions that are uppermost in the minds of Victorian and twentieth-century
Christians. Nothing, I suppose, has seemed more trouble-
some to people than the apparent contradiction between
the way things are described as happening in the Bible and
the account given of the same kind of phenomena by science. In the nineteenth century the theory of organic
evolution contradicted Genesis and shook men's faith; in
Spinoza's lifetime there was the apparent contradiction between the Scriptural geocentric universe and the Coper-
nican and Galilean heliocentric one. To Spinoza it presented no difficulty whatsoever: the power of prophecy
operated upon the imagination, not upon the intellect.
The certitude of prophecy is moral and the intuition or
imagination of the prophets can see many things not visi-
ble to the naked reason. But whatever they perceive is
within the framework of their own intellectual preconceptions. Joshua was a soldier, not an astronomer; when
the day appeared to him longer than usual, he explained
it as anyone else in his time would have explained it—that
the sun halted its movement across the sky. Indeed, it was
easy for Spinoza to demonstrate that even the greatest of
prophets, Moses himself, had a limited conception of the

nature of God: Moses' request that he might look upon the face of the Lord assumed that the Lord had a face, and even the reply that "No one shall look on Me and live" was not a denial of Moses' notion.[15] But the essential moral intuition of prophecy is no less valid because the theological or scientific guise in which it presented itself to the prophets was precisely their ordinary theological or scientific belief.

This line of reasoning is sufficient also to deal with the problem of divine inspiration of the Scripture as it appeared to popular Christianity in the nineteenth century, though Spinoza also set forth historically the process by which the so-called "canon" was established. To sum up: "As obedience to God consists solely in love to our neighbour—for whosoever loveth his neighbour, as a means of obeying God, hath, as St. Paul says (Rom. xiii. 8), fulfilled the law,—it follows that no knowledge is commended in the Bible save that which is necessary for enabling all men to obey God in the manner stated. . . . Other speculative questions, which have no direct bearing on this object, or are concerned with the knowledge of natural events, do not affect Scripture, and should be entirely separated from religion."[16] It is quite obvious that whoever has mastered this way of thinking has nothing to fear spiritually from the "higher criticism."

As for miracles, Spinoza is able to demonstrate that the popular conception of them is inconsistent not only with reason, but even with the Scriptural notion of a fixed and unchangeable order of nature and an unchanging God. Men, he says, call "the work of God, anything of which the cause is not generally known: for the masses think that the power and providence of God are most clearly displayed by events that are extraordinary and contrary to the conception they have formed of nature, especially if such events bring them any profit or convenience." A miracle is anything of which the cause cannot

be referred to the ascertained workings of nature, and recorded miracles are described in accordance with the understanding of the masses, who have made very little
progress in grasping fully the workings of nature. Indeed,
their only criterion is usually an appeal to memory; if
they recall something similar, they do not regard it with
wonder. But the very fact that we cannot understand a
miracle precludes its giving us an understanding of anything else because of it; indeed, if miracles were actually
events contrary to the laws of nature, they would demonstrate, if anything, that there was no God, for they would
cast doubt on the notion that nature followed a fixed and
immutable order, and that notion is fundamental to our
conception of God's existence. Moreover, those men—including the prophets—who have formed a conception of
God's providence that entails intervention on behalf of
certain human beings find themselves quite unable to rec-
oncile that conception with the order of nature and human affairs, "whereas philosophers who endeavour to understand things by clear conceptions of them, rather than
by miracles, have always found the task extremely easy—
at least, such of them as place true happiness solely in virtue and peace of mind, and who aim at obeying nature,
rather than being obeyed by her. Such persons rest assured that God directs nature according to the requirements of universal laws, not according to the requirements
of the particular laws of human nature, and that, therefore, God's scheme comprehends, not only the human
race, but the whole of nature." "The early Jews . . .
[tried] to show that the God whom they worshipped ar-
ranged the whole of nature for their sole benefit: this idea
was so pleasing to humanity that men go on to this day
imagining miracles, so that they may believe themselves
God's favourites, and the final cause for which God created and directs all things. What pretension will not people in their folly advance! They have no single sound idea

concerning either God or nature, they confound God's decrees with human decrees, they conceive nature as so limited that they believe man to be its chief part!"[17]

The denial of a special providence is of course an old doctrine, central to the Stoics and the Epicureans. When Arnold's Empedocles expresses it, he clearly is echoing Lucretius: "Picture a storm at sea. . . . Terrified, [the mariner] begs in his prayers that the winds may subside. . . . But in vain: no less for all his prayers is he borne by the violence of the hurricane to the shoals of death." If there really are personal gods to intervene in human affairs, Lucretius asks, why does not their lightning strike the outrageously immoral wretch, instead of, as so often happens, the man whose conscience is clear of sin? [18]

> *Streams will not curb their pride*
> *The just man not to entomb,*
> *Nor lightnings go aside*
> *To give his virtues room;*
> *Nor is that wind less rough which blows a good man's*
> *   barge.*
>
> *Nature, with equal mind,*
> *Sees all her sons at play;*
> *Sees man control the wind,*
> *The wind sweep man away;*
> *Allows the proudly-riding and the foundering bark.*

The way in which Arnold found Spinoza's view of miracles in the air in the early nineteenth century can be made clearer by putting side by side a passage from *Sartor Resartus* and one from *Literature and Dogma*. "The question of questions were," writes Diogenes Teufelsdroeckh: "What specially is a Miracle? To that Dutch King of Siam, an icicle had been a miracle. . . . 'But is not a real Miracle simply a violation of the Laws of Nature?' ask several. Whom I answer by this new question: What are the Laws of Nature? . . . Here too may some inquire, not without astonishment: On what ground shall one, that can make Iron swim, come and declare that therefore he can teach Religion? To us, truly, of the Nineteenth Century, such declaration were inept enough; which nevertheless to our fathers, of the First Century, was full of meaning." And Arnold: "What miracle of making an iron axe-head float on water, what successful prediction that a thing should happen just so many years and months and days hence, could be really half so impressive" as the moral and spiritual insights of Scripture? Yet the view of popular superstition was quite different: "Suppose I could change the pen with which I write this into a penwiper, I should not thus make what I write any the truer or more convincing. . . . But the mass of mankind feel differently." In their judgment, "could I visibly and undeniably change the pen with which I write this into a penwiper, not only would this which I write acquire a claim to be held perfectly true and convincing, but I should even be entitled to affirm, and to be believed in affirming, propositions the most palpably at war with common fact and experience." [19]

"Empedocles on Etna," as we have seen, was one of Arnold's earliest attempts to deal with modern religious problems from a naturalistic point of view, ridiculing faith in miracles, in an anthropomorphic God either hostile or benign, and finally in a future state of bliss.

> *Fools! That so often here*
> *Happiness mocked our prayer,*
> *I think, might make us fear*
> *A like event elsewhere;*
> *Make us, not fly to dreams, but moderate desire.*

The Carlylean tone of that last line is easily recognizable: "Blockhead! [thy misery] all comes of thy Vanity; of what thou *fanciest* those same deserts of thine to be. . . . *The Fraction of Life can be increased in value not so much by increasing your Numerator as by lessening your*

Denominator. . . . Make thy claim of wages a zero, then; thou hast the world under thy feet. Well did the Wisest of our time write: 'It is only with Renunciation (*Entsagen*) that Life, properly speaking, can be said to begin.' "[20]

But Arnold conceived that there was more to man's spiritual welfare than renunciation; hence his criticism of Carlyle many years later as being cut off from hope by his perverse attitude towards happiness. (Arnold's word for Carlyle earlier had been "moral desperado,"[21] by which I take it he meant the same thing.) "He fiercely attacks the desire for happiness; his grand point in *Sartor*, his secret in which the soul may find rest, is that one shall cease to desire happiness, that one should learn to say to oneself: 'What if thou wert born and predestined not to be happy, but to be unhappy!' He is wrong. . . . Epictetus and Augustine can be severe moralists enough; but both of them know and frankly say that the desire for happiness is the root and ground of man's being. Tell him and show him that he places his happiness wrong, that he seeks for delight where delight will never be really found; then you illumine and further him. But you only confuse him by telling him to cease to desire happiness: and you will not tell him this unless you are already confused yourself."[22] As he put it in "Obermann Once More":

> *The millions suffer still, and grieve,*
> *And what can helpers heal*
> *With old-world cures men half believe*
> *For woes they wholly feel?*
>
> *And yet men have such need of joy!*
> *But joy whose grounds are true;*
> *And joy that should all hearts employ*
> *As when the past was new.*

England had long remained in comfortable immunity to the poisonous theological doctrines emanating from

Germany, largely because, though the Church dominated education, theological studies as such either were neglected or looked back to such standard authorities as Paley and Bishop Butler. Laymen and amateurs showed themselves rather unskillfully aware that challenges were arising—laymen like Francis Newman, who in Arnold's view "wrote himself down an hass" with his *Phases of Faith*[23]—but these made only a slight stir among "advanced" thinkers and none at all within the Church. Then in 1860 a volume called *Essays and Reviews* appeared, seven long essays on aspects of Scriptural interpretation and ecclesiastical structure by seven authors, six of whom were clergymen (and among these, Arnold's personal friends Frederick Temple, Benjamin Jowett, and Mark Pattison). The essays were awkwardly done, long-winded, often unfortunate stylistically, but they were the work of intelligent men who had some scholarly equipment for the task, and they stirred up "confused alarms of struggle and flight" as ignorant armies clashed by night: for here at last the poisons seemed to have infected the Church itself, and there were even trials for heterodoxy.

Nearly two years later (1862), John William Colenso, bishop of Natal, published the first volume of his *Pentateuch and Book of Joshua Critically Examined*. Colenso had been an assistant master at Harrow and was best known as author of the most widely used school texts in arithmetic and algebra. He had made the gesture of publication which the Anglican church in the nineteenth century, like the American university in the twentieth, demanded, with some intellectually insignificant, relatively orthodox sermons, but when he was nominated to the missionary see in South Africa, he plunged himself with commendable zeal into the dissemination of Christianity among the African tribes, learned the Zulu language, and translated the Bible into that tongue. In the course of translating, he saw some aspects of the Scriptural account he had not noticed theretofore; like a good arithmetician, he added up his sums wherever they occurred, and found that the sums did not always come out right. Clearly, either God was an inferior arithmetician or God had not inspired the Bible; and in either case the foundations of faith were shaken and demolished. Honesty compelled him to publish his findings pell-mell; only a year before publication, as he candidly admitted in his Preface, he "had not the most distant idea of the results to which [he had] now arrived." His whole first volume, in fact, displays a most remarkable naïveté with respect to both religion and scholarship. As the *Times* summed it up: the bishop, with the help of "an intelligent Zulu, a sort of coloured Spinoza, as it would seem," set about his translation of the Bible. "This *enfant terrible* . . . began to ask impertinent questions, which Dr. Colenso found a difficulty in answering. . . . Instead of Dr. Colenso converting the Zulu, the Zulu converted Dr. Colenso." If "candidates for consecration should be examined in the Holy Scriptures," the *Times* concluded, there would be no "recurrence of this untoward affair."[24]

Every aspect of Colenso's book was vulnerable to ridicule, and so too were most of the comments upon it. The more intelligent critics found little admirable or disturbing about it; the popular, liberal press hailed it with enthusiasm. Colenso, undaunted by the ridicule, by the condemnation of his Metropolitan, the bishop of Cape Town, and by threats of trial for heresy, branched out from arithmetical demonstration to the natural sciences; whereas the dietary laws in Leviticus had named the hare as an animal that chews its cud, Colenso was able to publish in the *Times* an assurance from one of the leading naturalists of the day, Professor Richard Owen, that "the hare does *not* chew the cud; it has *not* the stomach of a ruminant animal."[25]

The whole circumstance stirred Arnold in his most sensitive part, his risibility. After all, Spinoza too had seen the arithmetical inconsistencies, and had dismissed them in two or three sentences; to him, and under his method of Biblical interpretation, they were insignificant. And so Arnold set about "contrasting Colenso and Co.'s jejune and technical manner of dealing with Biblical controversy" with Spinoza's.[26] Working sometimes as much as six or seven hours a day studying the authors he planned to deal with and ordering his materials, he had his article done and in the hands of the editor of *Macmillan's Magazine* within a month. His treatment of Colenso was devastating. "The Bishop of Natal's arithmetical demonstrations," he said ". . . are a series of problems, the solution of each of which is meant to be the *reductio ad absurdum* of that Book of the Pentateuch which supplied its terms. This being so, it must be said that the Bishop of Natal gives us a great deal too many of them. For his purpose a smaller number of problems and a more stringent method of stating them would have sufficed. It would then have been possible within the compass of a single page to put all the information which the Bishop's book aspires to convey to the mind of Europe." And then, adopting the form of a series of arithmetical "thought problems," reminiscent of Colenso's own textbooks, Arnold proceeded: "For example: if we take the Book of Genesis, and the account of the family of Judah there related—'*Allowing 20 as the marriageable age, how many years are required for the production of 3 generations?*' The answer to that sum disposes (on the Bishop's plan) of the Book of Genesis. Again, as to the account in the Book of Exodus of the Israelites dwelling in tents—'*Allowing 10 persons for each tent (and a Zulu hut in Natal contains on an average only 3 1/2), how many tents would 2,000,000 persons require?*' The parenthesis in that problem is hardly worthy of such a master of arithmetical statement as Dr. Colenso" (since a tent cannot contain half a Zulu); "but, with or without the parenthesis, the problem, when answered, disposes of the Book of Exodus. Again, as to the account in Leviticus of the provision made for the priests:

'If three priests have to eat 264 pigeons a day, how many must each priest eat?' That disposes of Leviticus." (Colenso had argued that a daily diet of 88 pigeons would be too much for any priest.) "Take Numbers, and the total of first-borns there given, as compared with the number of male adults: 'If, of 900,000 males, 22,273 are first-borns, how many boys must there be in each family?' That disposes of Numbers. For Deuteronomy, take the number of lambs slain at the Sanctuary, as compared with the space for slaying them: 'In an area of 1,692 square yards, how many lambs per minute can 150,000 persons kill in two hours?' Certainly not 1,250, the number required; and the Book of Deuteronomy, therefore, shares the fate of its predecessors. . . . Even a giant need not waste his strength."[27]

Spinoza, with a far keener apprehension of all aspects of the problem than Colenso, nevertheless had kept his eye accurately on the true function of Scripture; having cleared away the false firmly and economically, he directed attention to the valid and genuinely inspired moral insights that commanded faith and conduct. In Arnold's judgment, even the *Essays and Reviews*, though not intellectually naïve like Colenso's book, failed because they were neither scholarly enough nor able to show where the proper values of Scripture lay; his dislike for the hardline "higher critics" was to spring from the fact that they too, rigorous "systematizers" that they were, were entirely destructive. Once more Arnold picked up a favorite word of his father's and of Newman's as his criterion, the word "edifying."[28]

Arnold's sense of humor brought him, then, into the heart of the religious controversies of his day, this time in prose, not verse. A single article, however, would not suffice; another was needed to set forth Spinoza's doctrines more explicitly, and yet another, on the Stoic philosopher and emperor Marcus Aurelius, to convey a sense of how religion differs from simple morality. "Moral rules, apprehended as ideas first, and then rigorously followed as laws, are, and must be, for the sage only. The mass of mankind have neither force of intellect enough to apprehend them clearly as ideas, nor force of character enough to follow them strictly as laws. The mass of mankind . . . can be borne over the thousand impediments of the narrow way, only by the tide of a joyful and bounding emotion. . . . The noblest souls of whatever creed, the pagan Empedocles as well as the Christian Paul, have insisted on the necessity of an inspiration, a joyful emotion, to make moral action perfect; an obscure indication of this necessity is the one drop of truth in the ocean of verbiage with which the controversy on justification by faith has flooded the world. . . . The paramount virtue of religion is, that it has *lighted up* morality; that it has supplied the emotion and inspiration needful for carrying the sage along the narrow way perfectly, for carrying the ordinary man along it at all." And therefore the essay closes with its poetic image of Marcus Aurelius, yearning, as all such souls must yearn, for that something unattained by him, which when he saw it he did not recognize. "What an affinity for Christianity had this persecutor of the Christians! The effusion of Christianity, its relieving tears, its happy self-sacrifice, were the very element, one feels, for which his soul longed; they were near him, they brushed him, he touched them, he passed them by. . . . We see him wise, just, self-governed, tender, thankful, blameless; yet, with all this, agitated, stretching out his arms for something beyond,—*tendentemque manus ripae ulterioris amore.*"[29]

With this, Arnold again might have stopped. We have seen that he was drawn more and more into controversy with the political and social doctrines of the contemporary Liberals, and that he was motivated in part by a zest for controversy, in part by devotion to the cause of a public education that both the Millites and the Mialites opposed. In the England of the nineteenth century, however, one could not get to the bottom of the education question, nor of the Irish question, nor indeed deal with the structure and function of the State, without examining the question of Church Establishment.

In no respect, probably, was Arnold more at one with his father than in his conviction with regard to the spiritual and intellectual and social usefulness of the Church and his belief that its functions were best and most harmoniously performed if they were unified through an establishment. The enforcement of dogma was not at all Matthew Arnold's concern, though it was clear to him that the spiritual temper of all the Western world was controlled by the framework of the Judaeo-Christian Scriptures. He himself did believe in the values represented by the Scriptures and worked to preserve them, but even if he had not, he would have perceived their almost universal penetration into the spiritual life of society. Moreover, as I have pointed out more than once, Arnold had been brought up in an educational system that was almost exclusively in the hands of the clergy: the Established Church was at the heart of that system, and if one conceived that a concerted national effort was required for education, it was not at all unreasonable to believe that the best means of achieving that effort was through broadening and reforming the temper of the establishment rather than by throwing out the establishment altogether and having to set up something else. In one sense Arnold's support of the establishment was almost the equivalent of, let us say, our own advocacy of a National Endowment for the Humanities.

And therefore Arnold, when he was moderately well advanced in years, defined the Church of England in a lecture to its clergy as "a great national society for the promotion of what is commonly called goodness."[30] Much earlier he had alluded to Coleridge's conception, somewhat fanciful perhaps but well known also to Dr. Arnold, that "the whole body of men of letters or science formed the true clergy of a modern nation, and ought to participate in the endowments of the National Church."[31] Dr. Arnold himself had said, "My conviction of the benefits of a Church Establishment arises from this: that thus, and thus only, can we ensure the dispersion of a number of well-educated men over the whole kingdom, whose sole business, *is to do good of the highest kind*," and this included "instructing the young, visiting the sick, relieving, advising, and maintaining the cause of the poor; and spreading amongst all ranks the wholesome influence of a good life, a cultivated understanding, and the feeling and manners of a true gentleman."[32]

The Established Church, therefore, might be conceived as that aspect of the collective best self that was most concerned with the promotion of the spiritual and intellectual sides of culture. If powerful spiritual and intellectual forces existed outside the establishment, their absence from the collective effort was regrettable; but to the extent that they devoted their energies to combating the establishment, the consequence might be disastrous to the culture of the nation. And this appeared to be inevitable unless the current of nineteenth-century Liberalism could be in some way altered. In Arnold's judgment the alliance between Mialism and Millism, between Protestant Dissent and Utilitarianism, would end in disaster for the Mialites, since the new forces of the laboring classes were not rallying to the cause of Dissent; they were rallying to the cause of atheism and the denial of all traditional forms of spiritual and intellectual culture. No doctrine of Utilitarianism does Arnold recur to with more feeling than its notion that Christianity was merely sectarian, and the Established Church merely—and unjustly— the "dominant sect." [33] The only stratagem that would save either the Establishment or Dissent was to effect a re-alignment of forces—to effect an alliance of Dissent and Church against the common enemy, through comprehension of Dissent within the Church. Matthew Arnold, in deed, would have comprehended *all* churches, the entire spectrum from Unitarian to Roman Catholic, since his religion was entirely undogmatic; and he would have surrendered—as the Broad Church of his day was not yet inclined to do—government by episcopacy as the uniform mode of government within the Establishment. Having made clear, in *Culture and Anarchy*, the destructive effect of a divisive Dissent upon the spiritual life of the State, he set out almost immediately to demonstrate, first, that the dogmatic or doctrinal differences that distinguished the Protestant Dissenters from the Church were in fact not founded on a proper reading of Scripture (and especially of St. Paul's Epistles, upon which the Dissenters, whether Calvinist or Arminian or both, founded themselves), and, second, that historically, in England, the Church had always had a strong disposition (by no means uniformly prevailing, to be sure) toward Christian unity which should now dispose it to welcome the comprehension of Dissent and should dispose Dissent to regard the Church as its friend, not its enemy. *St. Paul and Protestantism* was the immediate sequel to *Culture and Anarchy*.

It is probably true that Arnold handled the doctrines of Dissent a little too rigidly in terms of their historical statements rather than their current force. When he cited the Racovian Catechism of Socinus for evidence of the doctrines of the Unitarians of the nineteenth century, the Unitarians protested that they had no historic connection with the Socinians and he changed his language. For Calvinism he went to the Westminster Confession and for Arminianism to the writings of Wesley, and when challenged with respect to the former he was able to point to the statement of doctrine currently and annually printed in the *Congregational Year Book*. His summary of the Westminster Confession is perfectly fair, yet his preservation of its legalistic language sounds to the modern reader like ridicule; indeed the Westminster Confession is so little in the consciousness of the modern Calvinists that a few years ago when a student in England asked a theologian who had recently written a book on Calvinism whether he could identify Arnold's statement, he replied that "it hardly sounds like Calvinism; it strikes me as a very crude statement."[34]

The interpretation of St. Paul's doctrines would inevitably, one might suppose, have involved Arnold in a full-scale attempt at Scriptural interpretation, if only to make clear what his own fundamental notions were; whether he could have brought himself to the task without the stimulus of his critics and his own delight in debate is not certain. But the critics came forward, critics who found "culture" as unsatisfactory a conception in religious matters as the radicals had found it in politics and sociology. One of Arnold's oldest friends, in especial, treated *Culture and Religion* in a series of lectures that dealt in succession with two of the greatest threats to Christianity (as the author saw it), "The Scientific Theory of Culture," represented by Huxley, and "The Literary Theory of Culture," represented by Arnold.[35] And so Arnold mapped out a reply, in the form of a series of articles—his usual form of publication—on "literature as it regards dogma; . . . literature as it regards physics" (i.e., natural science) and "literature as it regards science generally."[36] The articles as they developed proved too controversial for the editor of the magazine to tolerate and the series was broken off, but Arnold was embarked on the fulfillment of one of the central impulses of his life and he was not now to be stopped; he plunged into intense reading in theological matters and for more than a year devoted himself to *Literature and Dogma*, the only one of his prose works, apart from his reports on Continental education, that was written as a book rather than as a series of lectures or articles. It quickly became his most widely known book; its sale far outstripped his others and by the first decade of this century must easily have passed 100,000 copies. Today it is pretty much unknown, yet it has some claim to be regarded as the greatest work of his genius, at least in prose.

I have already indicated some of its fundamental positions with regard to dogma: God cannot be regarded as a person, and all reasoning based on such a notion is on a false track, including the notion that Jesus is the Son of God in any sense in which a father may be thought of as having sons, or that there is any meaning in the dogmatic concept of a Trinity. (Arnold was rather hard on the theologians who spoke of God as if he were "the man on the next street," and his rather flippant illustration of the popular conception of the Trinity as "the three Lord Shaftesburys" proved ultimately so much to distract outraged readers from his purpose that he abandoned it.[37]) The correspondence between New Testament fulfillment and Old Testament prophecy is to be explained on quite other than supernatural grounds; it is in some measure due to misreading, and in some measure to Jesus' conscious intention of altering the framework of the traditional Jewish Messianic thinking. Miracles simply do not happen, though we see how, when they are popularly expected, stories of them arise and are given credence. And the formulation and solidifying of dogma is a process that almost inevitably, throughout history, follows the disclosure of any profound insight into spiritual truth. All this, however, is negative, and Arnold's book is even more significant for its affirmation.

Much of the error of the New Testament record, or of the popular interpretation of it, arose from the simple fact that Jesus was over the heads of his reporters. He might therefore adapt his remarks to their way of thinking of things, or they might simply interpret his remarks in accordance with their own fixed patterns of thought. In an age in which physical illness was conceived to be

necessarily tied to moral sin—when the Jews could ask
Jesus, of a certain sick man, whether the man himself or
his parents had sinned—Jesus himself understood, perhaps
better even than the nineteenth century, the relation of
the mind to the body, and understood also how his followers would interpret any cure he effected. "What does
it matter whether I say, Thy sins are forgiven thee! or
whether I say, Arise and walk!" he asked his critics. Or
again, "Thou art made whole; sin no more, lest a worse
thing befall thee." [38] As Arnold's Empedocles said:

> *We would have misery cease,*
> *Yet will not cease from sin;*
> *We want all pleasant ends, but will use no harsh means.*

The story of the resurrection of Lazarus may well come
from the very attempt of Jesus to transform a popular
conception into a new and truer spiritual insight. Thus
Mary and Martha were convinced of the Pharisaical doctrine of eternal life in another world; when Jesus says,
"Thy brother shall rise again," Martha replies, "I know
that he shall rise again in the resurrection at the last day."
Whereupon Jesus makes his memorable statement of the
true spiritual insight that will provide a new life for all
his followers: "I am the resurrection and the life; he that
believeth on me, though he die, shall live, and whosoever
liveth and believeth on me shall never die." The story of
Jesus' own resurrection also comes from a combination of
the superstitious preconceptions of his followers with his
own perception of the impact his example will make on
them and the world, as when he says (to put together his
remarks as St. John recorded them in his fourteenth and
sixteenth chapters): "I go to the Father; I go, and come
again to you. A little while and ye see me not, and again
a little while and ye shall see me. I will not leave you
desolate, I will come to you. Yet a little while and the
world seeth me no more; but ye see me, because I live

and ye shall live."[39] I have already remarked the parallel in Empedocles' brushing aside the questions about the resurrection of Pantheia to raise the much more fundamental question of how man can transform his life in this world, and his ambiguous answer to Pausanias' question whether they should meet again in Catania.

Literature and Dogma aims at an understanding of the Bible that is acceptable to the modern mind; it must defend the Scripture against implications of fraud and deceit. It must also present a view of life that is harmonious with the insights of Scripture, and it must add the element of joy or emotion that distinguishes religion from morality or philosophy. The Spinozistic view of the universe, which is indeed also that of modern science, serves for a starting point: one does not look outside the system for any causes whatsoever of events within the system. Therefore, God may be defined, for purposes of modern science, as "the stream of tendency by which all things seek to fulfill the law of their being."[40] If the desire for happiness is the fundamental law of human nature, "our being's end and aim" (and Arnold takes it as axiomatic, turning from Carlyle to use the language of the Utilitarians against themselves), if in fact the fulfillment of our self-interest is compliance with the universal tendency, then we discover, with the help of Scriptural intuition, that Goethe's *Entsagen*, or "renunciation," is only partially valid; the universe is a moral universe, there is "something, not ourselves, that makes for righteousness," and therefore "to righteousness belongs happiness," "righteousness tendeth to life."

The great achievement of Jesus was to restore this intuition to a people that had lost it, and indeed to make the intuition available to all the world, by means of his method and secret. His method was inwardness, a concern for the state of one's own mind and conscience rather than for external and formal act; as Empedocles said,

84

Joy Whose Grounds Are True

Once read thy own breast right,
And thou hast done with fears;
Man gets no other light,
Search he a thousand years.
Sink in thyself! there ask what ails thee, at that shrine.

His secret was self-renunciation, and once again we hear echoes of Empedocles. Jesus carried self-renunciation beyond the cold advice of the moralists; it became for him a joyful dying to the forces of spiritual corruption and a rebirth into the new life of the "real self," that self that harmonized with the course of the universe; it caught the imagination of the world because he followed it even to the physical death of the cross. Others, however, have died for an ideal, even for a valid ideal; Jesus had one more virtue, his mildness and sweet reasonableness of temper. "This exquisite conjunction and balance, in an element of mildness, of a method of inwardness perfectly handled and a self-renouncement perfectly kept, was found in Jesus alone."[41]

Religion is morality touched with emotion; Jesus restored through his doctrine the emotion the Hebrews had always attached to morality, and he gave us the additional ground for emotion by providing himself as an object to which mankind could and did become attached through love and gratitude. Even the mystical doctrine of Christ's dying for our sins is profoundly and psychologically true. For if the just man, if Jesus, has no sins of his own to expiate, he must indeed, in this world, expiate the sins of his fellowman, of ourselves. "In truth, men's habitual unrighteousness, their hard and careless breaking of the moral law, do so tend to reduce and impair the standard of goodness, that, in order to keep this standard pure and unimpaired, the righteous must actually labour and suffer far more than would be necessary if men were better. In the first place, he has to undergo our hatred and persecution for his justice. In the second place, he has to make up for the harm caused by our continual shortcomings, to step between us foolish transgressors and the destructive natural consequences of our transgression, and, by a superhuman example, a spending himself without stint, a more than mortal scale of justice and purity, to save the ideal of human life and conduct from the deterioration with which men's ordinary practice threatens it. In this way Jesus Christ . . . 'suffered in our behoof,' 'bare the sin of many, and made intercession for the transgressors.' "[42]

It has always seemed paradoxical that Arnold so constantly affirmed his devotion to Cardinal Newman, even in the very books that took so opposite a course in the attempt to restore Christianity to the modern world. Arnold had already published nearly a third of *Literature and Dogma* when he wrote to Newman: "We are all of us carried in ways not of our own making or choosing, but nothing can ever do away the effect you have produced upon me, for it consists in a general disposition of mind rather than in a particular set of ideas. . . . I can truly say that no praise gives me so much pleasure as to be told (which sometimes happens) that a thing I have said reminds people, either in manner or matter, of you." (Newman replied that he was praying daily for Arnold's conversion.)[43] Arnold is entirely honest; Newman throughout his life had been constant to his conviction that the Scripture contained our most perfect body of true spiritual insight, and the example of Newman, like the example of his own father, undoubtedly gave Arnold his intellectual bias, prevented the loss of faith which befell so many of his contemporaries, and preserved his devotion to the spiritual intuitions of the Bible. Moreover, in his discussion of the development of Christian doctrine, Newman, with his basic conception that new times and new climates of thought reveal newer and truer ways of understanding doctrine, came close to Arnold's conception of the effect of the *Zeitgeist*; Arnold's method with all Christian writers was to try to grasp the essence of truth in them, as it shows itself to the modern spirit, and not to discard them out of hand because their way of seeing that truth necessarily differed from ours. Newman, like Arnold's own father, was by the accident of his time of birth prevented from using the language of the modern world, or even of seeing its true course. "[Papa] is the last free speaker of the Church of England clergy who speaks without being shackled, and without being obviously aware that he is so, and that he is in a false position in consequence," Arnold wrote to his mother. "I am quite sure Papa would have felt [this] had he been living now, and thirty years younger." And of Newman he said, "Born into the world twenty years later, and touched with the breath of the 'Zeit-Geist,' how would this exquisite and delicate genius have been himself the first to feel the unsoundness" of his traditional theological preconceptions.[44]

Arnold's own apprehension of the direction of modern thought with respect to the Established Church has probably not been borne out. But if one examines modern works of theology, one quickly perceives that Arnold anticipated very exactly the line of reasoning by which Christian thinkers would, rightly or wrongly, try to preserve their faith for the modern world. Only a few years ago a bishop in the Anglican Church tried to sum up the main currents of liberal theological thinking for the layman, in a book called *Honest to God*. I suspect Arnold would have regarded the title as one more sign that England was becoming—"to use a short and significant modern expression which every one understands,"—*Americanised*;[45] but if he had opened the book, he would have found paragraphs like these, from the same bench of bishops that in his own day was dedicated to "doing something for the honour of Our Lord's Godhead," to "the blessed truth that the God of the Universe is a Person":[46]

"We must . . . read the nativity story without assuming that its truth depends on there being a literal interruption of the natural by the supernatural, that Jesus can only be Emmanuel—God with us—if, as it were, he came through from another world. For, as supranaturalism becomes less and less credible, to tie the action of God to such a way of thinking is to banish it for increasing numbers into the preserve of the pagan myths and thereby to sever it from any real connection with history." "It is this union-in-estrangement with the Ground of our being . . . that we mean by hell. But equally it is the union-in-love with the Ground of our being, such as we see in Jesus Christ, that is the meaning of heaven. And it is the offer of that life, in all its divine depth, to overcome the estrangement and alienation of existence as we know it that the New Testament speaks of as the 'new creation.' This new reality is transcendent, it is 'beyond' us, in the sense that it is not ours to command. Yet we experience it, like the Prodigal, as we 'come to ourselves.' For it is a coming home, or rather a being received home, to everything we are created to be. It is what the New Testament can only call *grace.*"[47] Bishop Robinson does not mention Matthew Arnold in his book; Arnold's was the voice, not of a man, but of the Spirit of the Time.

Arnold again and again insisted that the method of literary criticism provided the only valid approach to Scripture, since the man of letters knew how to read imaginative works like the Bible—books written in a language that is literary, not scientific, "the language of poetry and emotion, approximative language, thrown out, as it were, at certain great objects which the human mind augurs and feels after, but not language accurately defining them." For all its transcendent value, moreover, the Bible was not unique; many others, poets and prophets, had insights into truth. Almost the highest expression of religious experience came from the pen of Sophocles.[48] And although the religion of Scripture is too much constricted in our day by its dogmatic interpretation, there is another path to religious intuition. "The reign of religion as morality touched with emotion is indeed indestructible. But religion as men commonly conceive it—religion depending on the historicalness of certain supposed facts, on the authority of certain received traditions, on the validity of certain accredited dogmas—how much of this religion can be deemed unalterably secure? . . . Our religion has materialised itself in the fact—the supposed fact; it has attached its emotion to the fact. For poetry the idea is everything; the rest is its world of illusion, of divine illusion; it attaches its emotion to the idea, the idea *is* the fact. The strongest part of our religion today is its unconscious poetry. The future of poetry is immense, because in conscious poetry, where it is worthy of its high destinies, our race, as time goes on, will find an ever surer and surer stay."[49] And once again we are back to the voice of Carlyle: "Religion, like all else [today], is conscious of itself, listens to itself; it becomes less and less creative, vital; more and more mechanical. Considered as a whole, the Christian Religion of late ages has been continually dissipating itself into Metaphysics; and threatens now to disappear, as some rivers do, in deserts of barren sand. . . . Literature is but a branch of Religion, and always participates in its character: however, in our time, it is the only branch that still shows any greenness; and, as some think, must one day become the main stem."[50]

Many claims have been advanced on behalf of Arnold. After all professors are a little like clergymen: they do not devote themselves to a writer without some conviction that he is worth the devotion; but if, in the end, the conviction has grown tepid, they dare not face the world without pretending that it is warmer than ever. What has most impressed me about Arnold, dealing closely as I have with his text and observing so intimately how he works, has been his remarkable gift for seizing upon precisely what he needs wherever he finds it. Those who belittle his acquaintance with philosophy are simply wrong, as his early reading lists—and his later ones—show. His curiosity was boundless, however, and so he read, not narrowly, but widely, and he wrote, not systematically, but practically. His point of view, which never changed, however much his reading and experience may have altered its applications, remained that of a temperamental transcendentalism adapted to a naturalistic, realistic frame of reference. When he had to work up a subject, as he did when he dealt with theology (but there is perhaps no better illustration of the point, in a more limited way, than one of his most neglected efforts, the tour de force *On the Study of Celtic Literature*), he read with a mind perpetually alert to whatever was useful in his sources, and then integrated his reading under the presidence of his fundamental point of view. This is not what we usually think of as originality; it is the wit to see what is of value in other, more original or more systematic, writers. Wit of another sort, allied through its comparable quickness of mind, he had in abundance: his tone of solemnity, so ill adapted to our temperament, was demanded by his age, but it seldom muffled, though it sometimes masked, the smile of the comic spirit. His description of himself as being in the main stream of modern thought was a fair estimate: one does not *make* the stream one floats in, but one may choose it. And so, in an age when the moral desperadoes might look to a past that could never be retrieved, when the liberals might lose sight of reality in claptrap and machinery, he perceived that though streams do not flow backward, though the modern spirit was necessarily liberal, yet nineteenth-century liberalism was hopelessly inadequate to the demands of humanity, socially, politically, and spiritually. By perceiving what elements of nineteenth-century liberalism gave promise for the twentieth century, he became, not only what he called Emerson, "the friend and aider of those who would live in the spirit," but the best representative, among the Victorians, of the modern spirit.

NOTES

Chapter I:
THE MAIN MOVEMENT OF MIND

1. Arnold, *Letters*, ed. G. W. E. Russell (London, 1895), II, 252 (January 18, 1884).
2. "A French Critic on Goethe," *Mixed Essays* (Arnold, *Works* [London, 1904], X, 264-65; *Prose Works*, ed. Super, vol. VIII).
3. G. R. Stange, *Matthew Arnold: the Poet as Humanist* (Princeton, 1967), pp. 213-48.
4. Arnold, *Essays, Letters, and Reviews*, ed. F. Neiman (Cambridge, Mass., 1960), p. 199; *Prose Works*, ed. Super, vol. VIII (address to the Royal Academy, May 1, 1875).
5. *Essays, &c.*, ed. Neiman, p. 308; *Prose Works*, ed. Super, vol. XI (address on his retirement, November 12, 1886).
6. Arnold, *Letters*, I, 27 (March 10, 1853).
7. For the composition of "Thyrsis," see Arnold, *Poems*, ed. K. Allott (London, 1965), pp. 496-98.
8. Arnold is mentioned as a past president of the Oxford Union in an article on its Jubilee in the *Times*, October 23, 1873, p. 5, col. 3.
9. See the account by one of Arnold's fellow scholars, reprinted in Arnold, *Letters to A. H. Clough*, ed. H. F. Lowry (London, 1932), p. 24.
10. Preface to *Essays in Criticism* (1865); *Complete Prose Works*, ed. R. H. Super (Ann Arbor, 1960–), III, 290.

11. "Lines Written on the Seashore at Eaglehurst," printed in *Poems*, ed. Allott, pp. 565–66.

12. "Emerson," *Discourses in America*, *Works* (1903), IV, 349–52; *Prose Works*, ed. Super, vol. X.

13. *Ibid.*, IV, 368. See "Marcus Aurelius" (1863), *Prose Works*, ed. Super, III, 156.

14. Carlyle, "Goethe" (1828); *Works*, Centenary ed. (New York, 1900), XXVI, 218, 243.

15. *Ibid.*, 208, 226, 247.

16. Almost in passing Arnold saw in that same essay of Carlyle's the question that provoked his early sonnet on Shakespeare: "Who knows, or can figure what the Man Shakespeare was, by the first, by the twentieth, perusal of his works? . . . His old brick dwellingplace, in the mere earthly burgh of Stratford-on-Avon, offers us the most inexplicable enigma."—*Ibid.*, p. 245. The passage is pointed out by Kathleen Tillotson, *Matthew Arnold and Carlyle* (London, 1956), p. 143n.

17. End of unpublished diary for 1847, now at Yale University; see *Letters to Clough*, p. 81. The passages from *Dichtung und Wahrheit* which Arnold transcribed into his notebook are printed in *The Note-Books of Matthew Arnold*, ed. H. F. Lowry, K. Young, and W. H. Dunn (London, 1952), pp. 446–57.

18. "Spinoza and the Bible" (1863); *Prose Works*, ed. Super, III, 176–77. The passage from Spinoza's *Tractatus* is in Chapter VI, 34.

19. "Goethe," *Works*, XXVI, 208. A friend of both Carlyle and Arnold, J. Llewelyn Davies, pointed out the resemblance between Arnold's and Carlyle's religious thought and the degree of their derivation from Goethe in a review of Arnold's *Literature and Dogma*.—"Mr. Matthew Arnold's New Religion of the Bible," *Contemporary Review*, XXI (May, 1873), 850–51.

20. "My dearest Clough these are damned times," wrote Arnold on September 23, 1849.—*Letters to Clough*, p. 111. Clough's two volumes were *The Bothie of Toper-na-Fuosich* and *Ambarvalia* (with Thomas Burbidge).

21. *Letters to Clough*, pp. 98–99, 97, 63, 65. The last sentence is awkward enough to make the reader uncomfortable,

without being certainly incomplete. It comes at the end of a leaf, has no punctuation after "matter," and may or may not be followed by the concluding portion of a letter on another kind of writing paper. If the second leaf belongs with the first, the word "matter" ends a sentence, since a new paragraph begins at the top of the second leaf. If the second leaf belongs to another letter, the conclusion of this letter is lacking and "matter" is perhaps not the last word in its sentence. One reader has made the perceptive suggestion that the context points to a reading "to unite matter with form."

22. "Matthew Arnold (by One Who Knew Him Well)," *Manchester Guardian,* May 18, 1888, p. 8. This unsigned article has been confidently (and surely correctly) attributed to Arnold's brother Thomas by Alan Harris, "Matthew Arnold: The Unknown Years," *The Nineteenth Century and After,* CXIII (April, 1933), p. 501. A much earlier, and presumably an informed, attribution to Thomas Arnold was by Florence Earle Coates, "Matthew Arnold," *Century Magazine,* XLVII (April, 1894), 937.

23. C. B. Tinker and H. F. Lowry, *The Poetry of Matthew Arnold: A Commentary* (London, 1940), p. 64. See also A. Dwight Culler, *Imaginative Reason* (New Haven, 1966), p. 38n.

24. Since "Mycerinus" seems to be capable of misinterpretation even by ordinarily competent scholars, who find "contradiction" between the first part of the poem and the second, or see in it "a poem that tacitly questions the existence of justice or of meaning of any kind in life," a word about what the poem is getting at may not be amiss, even though it has often enough, one would think, been adequately summarized. Mycerinus, the just son of a long-lived but unjust king, learns that he himself has only six years to live and proclaims with bitter irony that the gods, far from being the pattern from which men draw their notions of virtue, merely mock virtue:

> *The will*
> *Of the great Gods is plain; and ye must bring*
> *Ill deeds, ill passions, zealous to fulfil*

> *Their pleasure, to their feet; and reap their praise,*
> *The praise of Gods, rich boon! and length of days.*

And so he steps aside from the business of life to spend six years of revelry on an island in the Nile, and there, under the shadow of the prospect of death (which, after all, is the common human condition), learns the lesson that the reward of virtue is in being virtuous; other rewards, rewards men often expect in recompense for good deeds or in response to prayer, such as prosperity or long life, are irrelevant. The theme of the poem is in fact the education of the king. Like so many of Arnold's poems of about this time, "Mycerinus" handles by itself one of the many ideas brought together in the complexity of "Empedocles on Etna."

25. Arnold himself bore the cost of publication.
26. The manuscript is described in Tinker and Lowry, *Commentary*, pp. 8–16, and various passages are quoted *passim* (see their Index). It is the subject of a University of Rochester dissertation by David G. Osborne, *Matthew Arnold, 1843–49: A Study of the Yale Manuscript* (Ann Arbor, Mich.: University Microfilms, 1963).
27. The usual criteria for dating a manuscript on internal evidence—consistency of ideas with something we are able to date, or even repetition of a characteristic phrase used in a datable work—are especially untrustworthy in the case of Arnold, whose views throughout his mature life are remarkably homogeneous and in whom a characteristic expression very often reappears after a long lapse of time.

   I assume that a well-known sheet in T. J. Wise's collection, in the British Museum, was at one time in the sheaf now at Yale. It contains notes in ink about the career of Empedocles and a penciled version of "Dover Beach" without the last strophe, which is merely keyed in by reference. If Arnold himself separated this sheet of notes from the rest of his working papers, he may have done so in the latter part of 1853, since the 1853 Preface echoes the language of the notes. But very little is known of the provenance of either the "Yale Manuscript" or the Wise sheet; the separation (if they were at one time together) may have been made by a collector or bookseller. Of the light the Wise sheet throws on the dating of "Dover Beach," one can say: (1) Arnold was at work on the drama of "Empedocles on Etna" in the summer of 1849, and must therefore have assembled his materials—the penned notes—by that time; (2) "Dover Beach" can hardly have been written before Arnold's marriage in 1851, unless the "love" in the poem is someone other than his wife, or someone imaginary; (3) Arnold may still have had the penned sheet on his desk when he wrote the Preface of 1853, in view of the similarity of phrases; and (4) since the penciled "Dover Beach" is very unlikely to have been written at the same time as the ink notes on "Empedocles," it can as easily have been written on the sheet six years after those notes as two years after (or any other number). The only inference to be made from the manuscript, I think, is that the last strophe was already in existence before the rest of the poem was composed, and even this is only a probable, not a necessary inference. I have elsewhere remarked that it seems to me inconceivable that Arnold did not include "Dover Beach" in the collection he sent to the printer for publication in December, 1854, if it was ready by that time; one of the selling points of the *Poems. Second Series* was that it contained new material ("one-third of the volume is new," say the advertisements), and he would have wanted as much as possible—to say nothing about the self-discipline implied in withholding what he must have known was one of his very best poems. (The same argument does not hold for the 1857 volume, which was not a new collection but a third edition of the 1853 *Poems;* its only new poem was an addition to the already-existing "Switzerland" series. It has also been asserted that we have manuscript evidence that "Calais Sands," first published in 1867, was written in August, 1850, but in fact the manuscript does not tell us when the poem was written; its title, "By the Seaside near Calais. August, 1850," is meant to tell us when the event is supposed to have taken place. On Arnold's own testimony, the poem entitled "Rugby Chapel. November, 1857," was written as a reply to a criticism of Dr. Arnold that did not appear until 1858.) The British Museum manuscript is described in Tinker and Lowry, *Commentary*, pp. 289-90, 173-75. For "Calais Sands" and "Rugby Chapel," see Arnold, *Poems*, ed. Allott, pp. 233, 444.

28. Presumably Arnold alludes to the renaissance scholar Giordano Bruno and to F. D. Maurice. Schelling's *Bruno* —a philosophical dialogue in which Bruno is the principal speaker—appeared on one of Arnold's reading lists in the 1845 diary.

29. This is a summary of Spinoza's metaphysics.

30. See "Empedocles on Etna," lines 297-301:

> *And patiently exact*
> *This universal God*
> *Alike to any act*
> *Proceeds at any nod,*
> *And quietly declaims the cursings of himself.*

31. See the quotation from Arnold's letter to Clough, late 1847 or early 1848, above: "The poet's matter being *the hitherto experience of the world, and his own,* increases with every century."

32. There is no punctuation here. Did Arnold mean "There is no theory of life but is Stoical," or did he simply leave his sentence hanging without its key, and concluding, word?

33. This is the beginning of an old proverb that Arnold later quoted in *Literature and Dogma:* "If every one would mend one, we should have a new world."

34. The chief impetus for this idea seems to come from a letter J. C. Shairp wrote to Clough in July, 1849: "[Arnold] was working at an 'Empedocles'—which seemed to be not much about the man who leapt into the crater—but his name and outward circumstances are used for the drapery of his own thoughts. I wish Matt would give up that old greek form but he says he despises all the modern ways of going about the art and will stick to his own one." Tinker and Lowry thereupon observe in their *Commentary*, "Principal Shairp was quite right when he said that Empedocles was in a large measure Arnold himself." Shairp, it will be noted however, did *not* say that; to say that Ar-

nold's play used Empedocles' "name and outward circumstances . . . for the drapery of his own thoughts" is a very
different matter from saying that "Empedocles was in
a large measure Arnold himself." Some months after "Empedocles on Etna" was published, to be sure, Arnold
wrote to Clough: "Yes—*congestion of the brain* is what
we suffer from—I always feel it and say it—and cry for air
like my own Empedocles."—Tinker and Lowry, *Commentary*, pp. 287–88; Arnold, *Letters to Clough*, p. 130.

35. W. A. Madden, *Matthew Arnold* (Bloomington, Ind.,
1967), pp. 95, 99.

36. *Prose Works*, ed. Super, I, 1–2, 8, 13, or *Poems*, ed. Allott,
pp. 591, 598–99, 604.

37. Diogenes Laertius viii. 51–77. The verses are quoted in 62
and (with Latin translation) in *Empedoclis Agrigentini
Carminum Reliquiae*, ed. Simon Karsten (Amsterdam,
1838), II, 142–45. The latter book was Arnold's immediate
source.

38. Tinker and Lowry, *Commentary*, pp. 291–92.

39. *Ibid.*, p. 288.

40. Professor Allott remarks (so much in passing that one cannot be sure how significant he thought the point), "[Em-
pedocles'] ascent of the volcano . . . becomes a secular
Way of the Cross that ends in self-crucifixion."—"A Background for 'Empedocles on Etna,'" *Essays and Studies*,
XXI n.s. (1968), 94.

41. In *Literature and Dogma* Arnold wrote of the sister of
Lazarus: "Martha believed already in the resurrection of
Jewish and Christian *Aberglaube*. . . . But Jesus corrects
her *Aberglaube*, by telling her that her brother is not dead
at all; and his words, out of which the story of the miracle
[of the raising of Lazarus] very likely grew, do really
make the miracle quite unnecessary. 'He that has believed
on me and had my secret,' says Jesus, 'though his body
die to the life of this world, still lives; for such an one had
died to the life of this world already, and found true life,
life out of himself, life in the Eternal that loveth righteousness, by doing so.'

"Just in the same way, moreover, in his promise to
see his disciples again after his crucifixion and to take up

his abode with them, Jesus corrects, for those who have eyes to read, he corrects in the clearest and most decisive way those very errors, with which our common material conceptions of life and death have made us invest his death and resurrection. 'Yet a little while,' he says, 'and the world seeth me no more; but ye see me, because I live, and ye shall live too. He that hath my commandments and keepeth them, he it is that loveth me; and him that loveth me I will love, *and will manifest myself to him.*' Jude naturally objects: '*How* is it that thou wilt manifest thyself to us and not to the world?' And Jesus answers: 'If a man love me, he will keep my word, and my Father will love him, and *we will come unto him and make our abode with him.*' Therefore the manifestation of himself he speaks of is nothing external and material. It is,—like the manifestation of God to him that ordereth his conversation right,—the internal life and joy in keeping the commandments."—*Prose Works*, ed. Super, VI, 320–21. For Arnold's handling these same matters in *God and the Bible*, see Chapter III.

42. W. S. Johnson, *The Voices of Matthew Arnold* (New Haven, 1961), p. 108.

43. It is often said that Arnold's Empedocles begins his philosophical song with the assertion that man's soul is like a mirror spinning, impelled by the winds, along a cord slung through space. In fact, without pronouncing upon the absolute realities of the case, Empedocles insists that we cannot operate upon any such assumption:

> *Is this, Pausanias, so? . . .*
>
> *I will not judge. That man,*
> *Howbeit, I judge as lost,*
> *Whose mind allows a plan,*
> *Which would degrade it most.*

44. "Tennyson . . . one has . . . so in one's head, one cannot help imitating him sometimes," Arnold wrote to J. D. Coleridge on November 22, 1853.—Tinker and Lowry, *Commentary*, p. 83n. After Tennyson had published *In Memoriam* and succeeded to the laureateship, he was re-

garded as the spiritual guide for his age and was on that account so devastatingly characterized by the ironic stanza in "The Scholar-Gipsy":

> *Amongst us one,*
> *Who most has suffered, takes dejectedly*
> *His seat upon the intellectual throne;*
> *And all his store of sad experience he*
> *Lays bare of wretched days;*
> *Tells us his misery's birth and growth and signs,*
> *And how the dying spark of hope was fed,*
> *And how the breast was soothed, and how the head,*
> *And all his hourly varied anodynes.*
> *This for our wisest!*

45. Arnold's "Philomela," the only thing of its kind among his shorter poems, is actually of the same texture as the songs of Callicles.

46. Peter Bayne, "Mr. Arnold and Mr. Swinburne," *Contemporary Review*, VI (November, 1867), 342.

47. *Prose Works*, ed. Super, I, 2–3, or *Poems*, ed. Allott, p. 592.

48. An aside may serve to glance at the meaning of the final line of the poem, "And leave our desert to its peace," where "desert" is almost uniformly taken to signify some sort of barren, sandy waste. It means merely "isolated spot," with no suggestion of a state of vegetation in any way inharmonious with what has gone before. Arnold had good precedent for this use; Emerson, after describing the lush forest foliage near a pool where the redbird cools his plumage, alludes to the flowering rhodora as "pleasing the desert and the sluggish brook" because there are no people to see its beauty.

49. Heading of Book I, chap. x of *Sartor Resartus*.

50. *Works*, XXVIII, 31. The parallel was pointed out by K. Tillotson, *Arnold and Carlyle*, p. 149.

51. *Ibid.*, 32 (quoting the Preface to Jean Paul's *Hesperus*); Tillotson, p. 149.

52. *Prose Works*, ed. Super, VI, 383.

53. *Letters*, ed. Russell, II, 9 (June 5, 1869).

Chapter II:

THE LIBERAL OF THE FUTURE

1. *Apologia pro vita sua*, ed. M. J. Svaglic (Oxford, 1967), pp. 260–62 (Note A, "Liberalism").
2. *Note-Books*, ed. Lowry, pp. 440–45. R. C. Tobias, "On Dating Matthew Arnold's 'General Note-books,'" *Philological Quarterly* XXXIX (October, 1960), 426–34, inclines to date this Note-Book in the 1860's. He may be right as regards the entries from Burke, but some other entries are clearly datable from the late 1840's, through quotations from newspapers of those years.
3. "The Function of Criticism at the Present Time" (1864); *Prose Works*, ed. Super, III, 266.
4. E.g., in *A French Eton* (1864) and *Culture and Anarchy* (1868); *Prose Works*, ed. Super, II, 294, 377; V, 134–36.
5. "The Function of Criticism at the Present Time" (1864); *Prose Works*, ed. Super, III, 267–68.
6. *England and the Italian Question* (1859); *Prose Works*, ed. Super, I, 85.
7. *Culture and Anarchy* (1867–68); *Prose Works*, ed. Super, V, 135–36, 106.
8. Carlyle, *Works*, XXVII, 58. For Arnold's pride in his pairing of the terms, see *Prose Works*, ed. Super, VI, 420.
9. Carlyle, "Signs of the Times" (1829),"Jean Paul Friedrich Richter" (1827), *Works*, XXVII, 63; XXVI, 19–20. Arnold, *Culture and Anarchy* (1867), *Prose Works*, ed. Super, V, 93–94. The parallel was pointed out by D. J. DeLaura, "Arnold and Carlyle," *PMLA* LXXIX (March, 1964), 114, 122.
10. Carlyle, "Characteristics" (1831), *Works*, XXVIII, 10–11; DeLaura, "Arnold and Carlyle," p. 115.
11. *Prose Works*, ed. Super, III, 279–80.
12. "Heinrich Heine" (1863), *ibid.*, III, 108.
13. Carlyle actually anticipates Arnold's scorn of the willfulness of English scholarship and criticism. "Of Mr. Hope's new Book of Genesis, . . . of this monstrous Anomaly, where all sciences are heaped and huddled together, and the principles of all are, with a childlike innocence, plied hither and thither, or wholly abolished in case of need;

. . . what can we say, except, with sorrow and shame, that it could have originated nowhere save in England? It is a general agglomerate of all facts, notions, whims and observations, as they lie in the brain of an English gentleman; as an English gentleman, of unusual thinking power, is led to fashion them, in his schools and in his world: all these thrown into the crucible, and if not fused, yet soldered or conglutinated with boundless patience; and now tumbled out here, heterogeneous, amorphous, unspeakable, a world's wonder." So Arnold says of certain more recent works of English scholarship: "An extravagance of this sort could never have come from Germany, where there is a great force of critical opinion controlling a learned man's vagaries, and keeping him straight; it comes from the native home of intellectual eccentricity of all kinds,—from England, from a doctor of the University of Cambridge." Things of this sort "are of bad example. They tend to spread the baneful notion that there is no such thing as a high, correct standard in intellectual matters; that every one may as well take his own way; they are at variance with the severe discipline necessary for all real culture; they confirm us in habits of wilfulness and eccentricity, which hurt our minds, and damage our credit with serious people."—Carlyle, "Characteristics" (1831), *Works*, XXVIII, 35–36; Arnold, "The Literary Influence of Academies" (1864), *Prose Works*, ed. Super, III, 242–44.

14. Arnold, "A Recantation and Apology" (1869) and "Puritanism and the Church of England" (1870), *Prose Works*, ed. Super, V, 324, and VI, 101, with the notes on these passages; *Culture and Anarchy, ibid.*, V, 194–95.

15. Arnold, *Culture and Anarchy* (1868), *Prose Works*, ed. Super, V, 119–20, 131, and notes.

16. Arnold, "The Deceased Wife's Sister" (1869), *Prose Works*, ed. Super, V, 315, and note.

17. No expression of Arnold's has been more misunderstood by his casual modern critics than the word he so often used, "disinterestedness." "Disinterestedness" is viewing matters without preconceived and often irrelevant bias; it is the opposite of judging all things in terms of their su-

perficial bearing upon a single prejudice, or the profit of a group, as the Dissenters inclined to do in the matter of education. Disinterestedness is a far cry, however, from indifference; it calls to bear the highest play of the critical intellect, but it leads to convictions, and to the wish that those convictions should prevail.

Arnold defines "disinterestedness" again with respect to the study of the Bible as having "no foregone conclusion at the bottom of one's mind to start with, no secondary purpose of any kind to serve; but with the simple desire to see the thing, so far as this may be possible, as it really is."—*God and the Bible*, chap. iv, sec. 2, par. 2; *Prose Works*, ed. Super, vol. VII. The whole of the next paragraph elaborates this definition significantly.

18. Arnold, *Prose Works*, ed. Super, III, 484–85 (notes to the Preface to *Essays in Criticism*, 1865).

19. Epigraph to *Essays in Criticism* (1865), *ibid.*, III, 2.

20. "Signs of the Times" (1829), *Works*, XXVII, 58; *Sartor Resartus*, Book III, chap. v; "Characteristics" (1831), *Works*, XXVIII, 6. "The Schoolmen themselves are but the same false criticism developed, and clad in an apparatus of logic and system," said Arnold, *Literature and Dogma* (1873), *Prose Works*, ed. Super, VI, 348.

21. "Culture and Its Enemies" (1867), *ibid.*, V, 111.

22. "Anarchy and Authority" (1868) and Preface to *Essays in Criticism* (1865), *ibid.*, V, 504–5, and III, 289.

23. *On Liberty* (1859), "Introductory."

24. *Culture and Anarchy* (1868), *Prose Works*, ed. Super, V, 135.

25. Arnold, *Letters to Clough*, p. 68.

26. *Prose Works*, ed. Super, V, 217, 219.

27. *Ibid.*, II, 349, 362.

28. Kenneth Allott, "Matthew Arnold's Reading-Lists in Three Early Diaries," *Victorian Studies*, II (March, 1959), 258.

29. *Prose Works*, ed. Super, III, 136.

30. "Hellenism . . . has its more or less spurious and degenerated sub-forms, products which may be at once known as

degenerations by their deflexion from what we have marked as the flower of Hellenism,—'a kind of humane grace and artless winning good-nature, born out of the perfection of lucidity, simplicity, and natural truth.' And from whom can we more properly derive a general name for these degenerations, than from that distinguished man, who, by his intelligence and accomplishments, is in many respects so admirable and so truly Hellenic, but whom his dislike for 'the dominant sect,' as he calls the Church of England,—the Church of England, in many aspects so beautiful, calming, and attaching,—seems to transport with an almost feminine vehemence of irritation? What can we so fitly name the somewhat degenerated and inadequate form of Hellenism as *Millism?* This is the Hellenic or Hellenistic counterpart of Mialism; and like Mialism it has its further degenerations, in which it is still less commendable than in its first form. For instance, what in Mr. Mill is [but] a yielding to a spirit of irritable injustice, goes on and worsens in some of his disciples, till it becomes a sort of mere blatancy and truculent hardness in Professor Fawcett, in whom there appears scarcely anything that is truly sound or Hellenic at all."—Preface to *St. Paul and Protestantism* (1870), *ibid.,* VI, 126 and Textual Notes.

31. Pp. xxi–xxii; *Prose Works,* ed. Super, vol. VII.
32. "A Liverpool Address," *Five Uncollected Essays of Matthew Arnold,* ed. K. Allott (Liverpool, 1953), p. 91; *Prose Works,* ed. Super, vol. X.
33. "The Nadir of Liberalism" (1886), *Essays, &c.,* ed. Neiman, p. 269; *Prose Works,* ed. Super, vol. XI.
34. *Letters,* ed. Russell, I, 96 (June 25, 1859).
35. *On Liberty,* chap. ii (one-third through).
36. *Prose Works,* ed. Super, III, 145.
37. *On Liberty,* chap. ii; *Prose Works,* ed. Super, III, 144–45.
38. Macaulay, *History of England,* chap. vi (one-third through); Mill, *On Liberty,* chap. iv (end). But indeed, we need not look so far as Macaulay for expression of the Liberal distrust of the Jesuits; Mill himself said, "An individual Jesuit is to the utmost degree of abasement the slave of his order, though the order itself exists for the

collective power and importance of its members."—*On Liberty*, chap. v (near the end).

39. *On Liberty*, chap. ii (near the end); Arnold, *Culture and Anarchy* (1869), *Prose Works*, ed. Super, V, 244.

40. For Arnold on examinations for the very young, see *Schools and Universities on the Continent* (1868), *Prose Works*, ed. Super, IV, 92–93.

41. *Culture and Anarchy* (1868), *ibid.*, V, 154–55.

42. *On Liberty*, chap. v (two-thirds through).

43. *Schools and Universities on the Continent* (1868), *Prose Works*, ed. Super, IV, 313.

44. *Prose Works*, ed. Super, III, 535–36.

45. Arnold, *Note-Books*, ed. Lowry, p. 204 (Mill, *Autobiography*, chap. vi, near the beginning).

46. *Autobiography*, chap. v (four-fifths through).

Chapter III:
JOY WHOSE GROUNDS ARE TRUE

1. *Autobiography*, chap. ii (near the beginning).

2. Arnold, Preface to *Higher Schools and Universities in Germany* (1874), p. l; *Prose Works*, ed. Super, vol. VII. See Arnold, *Note-Books*, ed. Lowry, p. 204, and Mill, *Autobiography*, chap. ii (near the beginning and near the end). It is quite possible, however, that Mill was not inconsistent. Mill speaks of "the low moral tone of what, in England, is called society; the habit of, not indeed professing, but taking for granted in every mode of implication, that conduct is of course always directed towards low and petty objects; the absence of high feelings which manifests itself by sneering depreciation of all demonstrations of them, and by general abstinence (except among a few of the stricter religionists) from professing any high principles of action at all, except in those preordained cases in which such profession is put on as part of the costume and formalities of the occasion." If by this Mill means that the "stricter religionists" are distinguished from the rest only by their professions, not by their conduct, Arnold has misread him; and I incline to think this is the case.

3. *On Liberty*, chap. i (three-fourths through) and chap. ii

(eighth paragraph from the end), the latter cited by Arnold, "Marcus Aurelius" (1863), *Prose Works*, ed. Super, III, 133.

4. His younger brother Thomas suggests some temperamental division between Matthew and his father at the time of Dr. Arnold's death, but of what college freshman can this *not* be said?—[Thomas Arnold, jun.,] "Matthew Arnold (by One Who Knew Him Well)," *Manchester Guardian*, May 18, 1888, p. 8.

5. "Essay on the Right Interpretation and Understanding of the Scriptures," *Sermons* (4th ed.; London, 1845), II, 417, 379, quoted by E. L. Williamson, *The Liberalism of Thomas Arnold* (University, Ala., 1964), pp. 78, 93; and see Williamson, pp. 79, 81–82, 92.

6. E. H. Coleridge, *Life and Correspondence of John Duke Lord Coleridge* (London, 1904), I, 122 (letter from M. Arnold to J. D. Coleridge, January 8, 1843). The same letter expresses warm admiration for Newman.

7. Edward Walford in a letter to the *Times*, Friday, April 20, 1888, p. 13, quoted in Arnold, *Letters to Clough*, ed. Lowry, p. 24.

8. *Letters to Clough*, p. 117; K. Allott in *Victorian Studies*, III (March, 1960), 320; T. Arnold, "Matthew Arnold," *Manchester Guardian*, May 18, 1888, p. 8.

9. W. H. G. Armytage, "Matthew Arnold and T. H. Huxley," *Review of English Studies*, IV n.s. (October, 1953), 350.

10. S. T. Coleridge, *Biographia Literaria*, ed. J. Shawcross (Oxford, 1907), II, 217 (end of chap. xxiv); Arnold, *Prose Works*, ed. Super, III, 415–16, 57.

11. "Stanzas in Memory of the Author of 'Obermann,' " lines 57-60.

12. An excellent discussion of his philosophy is Stuart Hampshire's *Spinoza* (Harmondsworth: Penguin Books, 1951).

13. *Tractatus Theologico-Politicus* xiv, 30–32, 37–38, tr. R. H. M. Elwes. See Arnold, "The Bishop and the Philosopher" (1863), *Prose Works*, ed. Super, III, 167.

14. D. J. DeLaura, "Matthew Arnold and John Henry Newman," *Texas Studies in Literature and Language*, VI (Supplement, 1965), 671 (letter of January 3, 1876).

15. *Tractatus* ii, 26–27, 42; see Arnold, *Prose Works*, ed. Super, III, 162-63.

16. *Tractatus* xiii, 8, tr. Elwes; see Arnold, *Prose Works*, III, 166.

17. *Tractatus* vi, 1, 34, 4–5, tr. Elwes; see Arnold, *Prose Works*, III, 168–69, 176.

18. *De rerum natura* v, 1226–32, vi, 387–95. Lucretius much admired the philosopher Empedocles.

19. *Sartor Resartus*, Book III, chap. viii ("Natural Supernaturalism"); Arnold, *Literature and Dogma* (1873), *Prose Works*, ed. Super, VI, 392, 245.

20. *Sartor Resartus*, Book II, chap. ix ("The Everlasting Yea"). The parallel is pointed out by K. Tillotson, "Arnold and Carlyle," pp. 144–45.

21. Arnold, *Letters to Clough*, p. 111 (September 23, 1849).

22. "Emerson" (1883), *Works* (1903), IV, 378; *Prose Works*, ed. Super, vol. X. See K. Tillotson, "Arnold and Carlyle," p. 146. The quotation from *Sartor* is from Book II, chap. ix ("The Everlasting Yea"), the paragraph following that quoted above.

23. *Letters to Clough*, p. 115 (May, 1850).

24. Colenso, *The Pentateuch and Book of Joshua Critically Examined*, Part I (New York, 1863), p. 12 (Preface); *Times*, February 16, 1863, p. 8, col. 4.

25. *Times*, April 2, 1863, p. 10, col. 6.

26. Arnold, *Letters*, ed. Russell, I, 176 (November 19, 1862). See also *Prose Works*, ed. Super, III, 415.

27. "The Bishop and the Philosopher" (1863), *Prose Works*, ed. Super, III, 48.

28. *Ibid.*, III, 53–54.

29. "Marcus Aurelius" (1863), *ibid.*, III, 134, 156–57.

30. "The Church of England" (1876), *Last Essays on Church and Religion*, *Works* (1904), IX, 345; *Prose Works*, ed. Super, vol. VIII.

31. "The Bishop and the Philosopher" (1863), *Prose Works*, ed. Super, III, 51.

32. T. Arnold, *Miscellaneous Works*, ed. A. P. Stanley (London, 1874), pp. 219–20, quoted by Williamson, *The Liberalism of Thomas Arnold*, p. 126. The force of Dr. Arnold's concern for an establishment—but a comprehensive

establishment that would include all sects—is interestingly revealed in a long letter Clough wrote to his sister while he was still a schoolboy at Rugby, in which, as was very likely to happen when the matter of an establishment arose in those circles, the bad example of the United States was held up as negative evidence.—*The Correspondence of Arthur Hugh Clough*, ed. F. L. Mulhauser (Oxford, 1957), I, 33 (December 30, 1835).

33. *Literature and Dogma* (1873), *Prose Works*, ed. Super, VI, 148; *St. Paul and Protestantism* (1870), *ibid.*, VI, 126.

34. Reported by Miss Jean A. Smallbone in her unpublished M.A. dissertation, "*St. Paul and Protestantism:* Its Place in the Development of Matthew Arnold's Thought" (University of London, 1950).

35. The friend was J. C. Shairp, who was at Balliol College with Arnold. For other stimulants to the writing of *Literature and Dogma*, see William Blackburn, "The Background of Arnold's *Literature and Dogma,*" *Modern Philology*, XLIII (November, 1945) 130–39.

36. *Prose Works*, ed. Super, VI, 538.

37. See *Prose Works*, ed. Super, VI, Index *s.v.* "Shaftesburys."

38. *Literature and Dogma* (1873), *ibid.*, VI, 254–55.

39. *Ibid.*, VI, 320–21; *God and the Bible* (1875), chap. vi, sec. 7 and 3, *Prose Works*, ed. Super, vol. VII.

40. "St. Paul and Protestantism" (1869), *Prose Works*, ed. Super, VI, 10; "Literature and Dogma" (1871), *ibid.*, VI, 195–96.

41. *Literature and Dogma* (1873), *ibid.*, VI, 300.

42. "St. Paul and Protestantism" (1869), *ibid.*, VI, 66.

43. Arnold, *Unpublished Letters*, ed. A. Whitridge (New Haven, 1923), pp. 56–57 (November 29, 1871). For Newman's remark, see DeLaura, "Arnold and Newman," p. 671 (it was not an immediate reply to Arnold's letter, but was written in response to some later gifts of books).

Fifteen months after Arnold's letter to Newman, R. H. Hutton, reviewing *Literature and Dogma* anonymously in *The Spectator*, commented upon one passage (*Prose Works*, ed. Super, VI, 386:27–387:15): "It is impossible to doubt that the man who wrote that fine passage,—a passage reminding us, both in its wording and its liquid rhythm, of many a passage in Father Newman,—has a profound sympathy with the teaching of the Bible." —February 22, 1873, p. 243.

44. Arnold, *Letters*, ed. Russell, I, 177–78 (December 17, 1862); *Literature and Dogma* (1873), *Prose Works*, ed. Super, VI, 377. Professor Trilling quotes from Goethe: "The age [is] the force which hurries him, whether willing or unwilling, along with it, guiding him, moulding him; so that one may venture to pronounce that the fact of being born ten years earlier or later would have made a man an entirely different person as regards his own development and his influence on others."—*Matthew Arnold* (New York, 1939), p. 36.

45. "Democracy" (1861), *Prose Works*, ed. Super, II, 16.

46. *Literature and Dogma* (1871–73), *ibid.*, VI, 166, 267.

47. J. A. T. Robinson, *Honest to God* (Philadelphia: The Westminster Press, 1963), pp. 68, 80.

48. *Literature and Dogma* (1871–73), *Prose Works*, ed. Super, VI, 243 *et passim*. For Sophocles' expression of the religious experience, see *ibid.*, VI, 178, 195 and "Pagan and Mediaeval Religious Sentiment" (1864), *ibid.*, III, 231.

49. Introduction to the section on Poetry in *The Hundred Greatest Men* (1879), *Essays*, &c., ed. Neiman, p. 239; *Prose Works*, ed. Super, vol. IX. Arnold quoted this passage again in "The Study of Poetry" (1880), *Essays in Criticism*, second series (beginning).

50. "Characteristics" (1831), *Works*, XXVIII, 23. Arnold's famous statement has also been linked to a passage in one of Newman's sermons.—D. J. DeLaura, "Arnold and Newman," p. 683, citing Denis Butts, "Newman's Influence on Matthew Arnold's Theory of Poetry," *Notes and Queries*, CCIII (June, 1958), 255–56. No doubt parallels could also be found elsewhere. Like so many of the ideas dealt with in these lectures, it was probably more widely current than the modern reader of one or two books might suppose. Newman, of course, read Carlyle.

INDEX

A reference to a page of text should be taken to include the notes to that page.

Index

Index

Harrow, 73
heaven, 23, 25, 62, 71, 88
Hebrews, Jews, 65–66, 69, 75, 82–83, 85, 99
Heine, Heinrich, 35
Hellenism, 104–5
history, 32, 53–54, 63, 68, 80, 82, 88–89
Homer, 16, 19, 23
Houghton, W. E., ix
Humboldt, Wilhelm von, 57
Hutton, R. H., 109–10
Huxley, T. H., 65, 81

"idea of the world," 12, 14, 25
idealism, 11, 58; *see also* transcendentalism
immortality, 20, 83, 99
Independents, 55
industry, 34–35, 42, 50, 55, 79
intuition, 23, 58–59, 67–68, 82, 84, 86, 89
Ireland, 40–42, 52, 78
Italy, 26

Jesuits, 54–55, 105–6
Jesus, 22, 28, 40, 64, 82–86, 88, 99–100
Jobson, F. J., 40, 42
Johnson, W. S., 22
Joshua, 67, 73
Jowett, Benjamin, 73
joy, 11, 16, 21, 26, 28, 31, 69, 71–72, 77, 84–85
Judah, 75
Jude, 100
justification by faith, 77

Karsten, Simon, 99
King, Martin Luther, assassination, viii
Kinglake, A. W., 39
knowledge, 11, 18, 31, 49, 56, 68

Lake District, 12
Lansdowne, Henry, Marquis of, 11, 14, 32
Lazarus, 22–23, 83, 99
Lessing, G. E., 10

Leviticus, 74–76
liberalism, Liberals, Whigs, 11, 31–32, 34–36, 38, 40–44, 46, 48–52, 54–55, 59, 74, 77, 79, 87, 90–91, 105
Licensed Victuallers, 56–57
literature, 4, 33, 35, 81, 88–89
Liverpool, 52
London, 11, 32, 48–49; University College, 47
Lowe, Robert, 50
Lowry, H. F.: *see* Tinker, C. B., and Arnold, *Letters to Clough*, *Note-Books*
lucidity, 52, 105
Lucretius Carus, T., 22, 28, 70, 108

Macaulay, T. B., 39, 55, 105
machinery, mechanical, 24, 37–38, 46, 58–59, 89–90
Macmillan's Magazine, 75
Madden, W. A., ix, 18
Manchester Guardian, 95, 107
Marguerite, 3
Mary and Martha, sisters of Lazarus, 83, 99
Marylebone Vestry, 48
materialism, 24, 28, 31, 37, 89
Maurice, F. D., 15, 27, 98
messianism, 82
Methodists, 40
Mialism, 36, 39, 50–52, 77, 79, 105
Miall, Edward, 36
middle class, 34–35, 38–39, 42, 49
Mill, Harriet, 59
Mill, James, 36
Mill, J. S., x, 36, 47–48, 50–53, 59, 61–62, 105; *Autobiography*, 59, 61–62, 106; *On Liberty*, 48, 50, 53–59, 62, 105–6
Millism, 36, 51–52, 77, 79, 105
Milwaukee, 1
miracles, 22, 25, 63–64, 68–71, 82–83, 99
modern ideas, spirit, 18–19, 24–25, 29, 34–36, 47, 52–54, 63, 66–67, 71, 84, 86–87, 90–91, 98

115

Index